# INSIDE C
# LOCOMOTIVE WORKS

## 1942 to 1992

## My 50 years in the Workshops

### With many photographs from LNWR, LMS & BR eras

## by Bryan Skellon

### and Neil Smith

Published in the United Kingdom 2018

By Roxby Publications

Copyright © 2018

Bryan Skellon

ISBN 978-0-9556232-2-6

Special Note from the author:

Any surplus from the sales of this book will be donated to

St. Luke's (Cheshire) Hospice

# INTRODUCTION:

This is a compilation of long-gone work conditions and experiences throughout my employment in Crewe Railway Workshops, over 50 fascinating years, 1942 to 1992.

From the age of 14 to 63 is a long time to be employed by one company, but that was normal in pre-war and post Second World War conditions. Everyone who entered railway employment expected a job for life – so very different from the modern day short-term work contracts.

One of the remarkable things about such long-term employment was the process of growing up with your workmates beside you; starting work with boys as apprentices, seeing them getting married, then having families - and all the while keeping in close contact with them up to the day of their retirement.

Fathers, sons, uncles, brothers and grandfathers would work in close proximity to one another - sometimes in the same department - so it would be possible to know quite a lot of the family's business; where they lived, where their local pub was and even what beer they drank which, by the way, was one of the main topics!

From a flood of memories, I hope the following chapters describe the many good moments as well as the sometimes unfortunate events that occurred in my working life.

The reader will realise that Health and Safety laws are only a comparatively recent requirement in this country and that conditions of work in my early days in Crewe Works were often extremely hard and sometimes hazardous and dangerous in the extreme.

In the first chapter I describe my early life in Crewe which gives an indication of the living and social conditions leading up to the Second World War.

Bryan Skellon - Apprentice

# Acknowledgements:

Thanks go to my friend Neil Smith who fully revised and edited my original story which was written for my family. Also to Sue Brown who typed the manuscript. Special thanks to Roy David for help and advice during final editing.

I am also grateful to the following for use of photographs: Manchester Locomotive Society, LNWR Society, Crewe Family History Unit, Crewe Heritage Centre, Chris Thorley and Neil Smith.

Cover Design: Neil Smith

Printed by Printdomain

# CHAPTER 1
## My early life in Cheshire

I was born in Hall Lane, Warmingham, Cheshire, on 28th August 1928 and christened John Bryan, son of John and Elizabeth Skellon. My brother Roy had sadly died at the age of five from meningitis (at that time no cure was possible as there were no antibiotics and penicillin itself was not developed until the 1940s). It was a terrible blow to my parents and, as you can imagine, my mother took years to get over the shock.

When I was two the family moved to Crewe. My Mother related to me an incident which occurred when I was about three. It was washing day and she had locked me in the parlour with my toys to keep me out of mischief. She had earlier lit the boiler fire and while attending to me put the box of matches she had used in a nearby cupboard. Sometime later she smelled smoke and thought at first it was from the boiler. But to her subsequent horror she could see the smoke was coming from under the parlour door. On opening it she was met by a wall of smoke from a blazing sofa. And there was me lying on my stomach watching the flames with great childish curiosity. I was very lucky to have escaped with my life from such self-imposed danger.

Then, when I was almost four, I found myself lying in a bed in Crewe Cottage Hospital with a very painful abdomen - peritonitis, which was extremely serious for a child. Our family doctor, Dr English, performed the operation himself but, owing to the severity of the infection, was forced to warn my parents that I had very little chance of recovery. I vividly remember the amount of tubes which were inserted into me to drain away the dreadful poison. These were covered in thick wadding which was painfully removed and replaced every morning. I was not allowed visitors for six weeks and I

5

remember my dad had to just look through a small window near my bed and wave to me. I was in hospital for 12 weeks all told, gradually regaining my strength. The medical costs for the operation and for the family's treatment was regularly collected by the 'Doctor's Man' as my mother called him…four shillings, the equivalent of 20p per week.

One day my dad took me on an outing to a zoo in the nearby village of Shavington. We got there on his bike with me on the crossbar. After seeing some of the various animals we came to the chimpanzees which were one of my favourites. Dad gave one of them a bar of chocolate which seemed to have been gratefully accepted. I was delighted when the chimp came close up to the bars of the cage chewing away merrily. But, all of a sudden, the chimp spat out a great spray of chocolate all over dad's Sunday-best light fawn suit. We returned home a lot quicker than the outward journey without a word being said. From then on Zoo visits were banned.

My sister Joyce once took me to the Empire cinema in town. I remembered it for two reasons; firstly it was a long walk for my little legs and secondly the visit ended abruptly. The picture had only just started when, as part of the film, a huge mass of flames appeared on the screen. Joyce grabbed me by the arm and dragged me outside because she thought the cinema was on fire!

I went to Adelaide Street Infant's School which was just around the corner from the shop in Broad Street where we lived. Many times I would run home when I had the chance to escape - but my Mother always dragged me back after a smack on the bottom.

In 1933, at the age of five, the family – father, mother and sisters Joyce and Iris moved to a cottage in Waldrons Lane, Coppenhall, where I was to spend the next 15 years. This was a new experience, living in the country with plenty of open fields to play in and many new friends. My journey to school (mostly on my own) was about a mile but seemed a very long walk. The route was partly by footpath through fields skirting around cows and horses. In winter it could be very frightening and on one occasion running home after dark in driving rain I fell over a horse lying on the path which really scared me.

About this time my mother was knocked down by a motor car. She was cycling through a crossroads on the way to town when the vehicle failed to stop at a halt sign and hit her side on. She landed on her knees which were badly cut. She was taken to hospital by another motorist where they stitched and patched her up and she had to spend a month in bed before she was fully recovered. In contrast to today, no police were involved and there was no talk of any compensation - but this seemed to be normal in those days.

Waldrons Lane was a meeting place for gypsies. As many as eight caravans would be parked in the field next to our house. One gypsy family, the Watsons, had a permanent spot and were very nice people. But the majority were very rough – the kids were often unwashed, poorly dressed and cruelly treated by their parents. They only had the most basic things. I used to chat to them and sometimes visit their vans where I could see the extent of their hard living conditions. Their main diet was rabbit which were caught by their greyhounds. I saw them collecting pigeon's eggs and eating them raw. Hedgehogs were trapped, then wrapped in clay and roasted on the open fires. Once, I saw one that was being prepared for eating by removing the clay which in turn pulled out the prickles and peeled off the skin – it looked horrible to me.

The kids slept under the caravans which had tarpaulins wrapped around the wheels to protect them from the cold winds. Many times when going past to school on winter mornings I used to wonder how they kept warm. The adults, of course, were tucked up in their nice cosy stove-heated vans.

As I got older I had many interests. Collecting birds' eggs was one – a pastime every country boy pursued. I climbed trees for hawk, crow and ravens' eggs and waded into pools and ponds to collect water fowl eggs. I pierced them with a thorn at both ends and blew out the contents and then packed them into a box lined with cotton wool for safe keeping on the way home.

On one occasion, some friends and I decided to make a raft hoping to take some swans' eggs from a nest on an island in a nearby pool. We carried six five-gallon sealed cans and a number of wooden spars to the poolside and started assembling it there, all lashed together with some rope – it presented a very shaky structure indeed. After a very wobbly launch, two of us started the outward journey paddling with our hands.

As we neared the island the cob (male) swan, who was obviously guarding the nest, began to get agitated. The next instant in a flurry of spray and feathers, he rapidly headed in our direction. In our attempt to put the raft into a quick reverse gear, our prized vessel capsized. We somehow managed to cling onto the spars and frantically tread water until we finally arrived back on dry land. Soaked to the skin and covered in mud, we reviewed the situation and decided we'd better leave swans well alone in future. Egg collecting is against the law now, of course, and so it should be – but I am talking here about the 1930s.

Before the Second World War, boys very rarely committed vandalism. The punishment for it and other criminal acts was very harsh. The Birch, a bunch of thick yard-long twigs tied together, was administered to young boys for minor offences – as many as twelve strokes at a time. The Cat O'Nine Tails was another form of punishment. This was a whip with nine leather thongs used on teenagers and adults. It would badly cut and bruise the bared back.

The other form of punishment was a spell in a reformatory school where children up to the age of 16 were subjected to a rigorous regime of discipline. A boy I knew well, who was 12, shot an airgun pellet through the keyhole of a door hitting a girl in the eye. For this offence he received six strokes of the birch and three years in a reformatory school.

The cottage where we lived was quite basic. There was no flush water toilet – just a couple of tins with seats, one large seat for the adults and a small seat for the children situated in a brick shed outside. There were no electric lights – only oil lamps. We had no bathroom so we had one bath a week in a tin bath which was placed in front of the living room fire in cold weather.

Mother would heat the bath water in a coal fired boiler in the kitchen and this was also used on washing day for boiling the dirty clothes. There was also a huge earthenware sink alongside the boiler with just a cold tap. There was no hot and cold running water in those days! The only fire was in the living room with an oven on the side for cooking and baking. A kettle was hung over the fire to boil water for making tea. You can imagine in very cold weather with only one fire the whole house was like an ice box.

I was 11 in 1939 when the Second World War commenced and had just started at senior school. I was always in the 'A' stream although I was not a brilliant scholar. Nothing much happened at school apart from three memorable events: the first was the black eye given to me by the woodwork master for carving my name in the workbench. When I told my dad he just said 'it serves you right'.

The second was when I took a military shell fitted with a wooden bullet to show my teacher. I had picked it up from the town hall steps in Crewe where it had been left by the Cambridgeshire Regiment after a mock battle with the Crewe Home Guard and Fire Service. The teacher placed it on an anvil and hit the firing pin with a hammer. The classroom was immediately engulfed in dense blue smoke and ended with the pupils, teacher and me crawling on our hands and knees out of the room gasping for breath.

In the early years of the war my cousin and I used to collect tail fins from incendiary bombs which were directed at Crewe but had fallen in the surrounding countryside. We also found parachutes which had been used to carry land mines.

Everyone, both adults and children, was issued with a gas mask. Every child would carry their gas mask in a tin to and from school slung around their neck on a cord. My cord was so long that the tin rattled my legs as I walked. Every day we would put them on for five minutes to get familiar with them. Corrugated-iron air raid shelters were provided for all disabled people which, because my dad had a disablement, meant we had one. During the many air raids we suffered, the shelter was filled with the neighbourhood's womenfolk and children with my dad and the other men standing outside.

It was frightening to be woken up by the sirens and then a few minutes later to hear the German bombers with their distinctive intermittent engine sound flying over Crewe. Bombs were dropped on Crewe Railway Works and Rolls Royce and there were a lot of casualties – many were injured and many died.

Once in the middle of the night I heard a terrible screaming sound from very close by which seemed to fill the whole bedroom. I was out of bed nearly as quick as the tremendous thump which followed. I found out the next day that it was a whistling bomb dropped by a German bomber. It landed about 300 yards from our house in a field off Moss Lane and, fortunately, failed to explode.

I left school at the age of 14 in 1942 and started work at a farm in Elworth a couple of miles from home. The work was hard, especially for me, a skinny boy, thin as a rake. But the outdoor life toughened me up. This was for a short period of six months until I was accepted for an apprenticeship in the Crewe Locomotive Works. My first job on the farm was to trim a hedge about ¼ mile long. What a first job – it took me about a month through rain, hail and snow!

The farmer I worked for was a cattle dealer who bought his cattle from Ireland where they had been bred on the bogs. They had never been handled before and were as wild as deer. They would arrive at Sandbach station every Thursday. After they had been unloaded from the cattle wagons I and Victor (an Italian prisoner of war) would walk them to the farm in Elworth. I say walk, but they were off into gardens or going the wrong way with both of us running about desperately trying to drive them in the right direction. The trauma wasn't finished when we had them chained up in the shippons - they had to be milked. What an effort it was – these cattle had never been inside before and were jumping all over the place. When attempting to milk them they would kick out viciously so we had to strap their back legs together. Even fitting the straps was a danger.

# CHAPTER 2

## Life as a Works' apprentice

So, at the tender age of 14 years and 6 months, I started my apprenticeship in the London Midland and Scottish Railway Works in Crewe. This meant I would spend periods in each of the works departments learning differing skills and trades until, at the age of 21, I would become a recognised skilled tradesman.

I was fortunate in a way because if your father was not employed by the railway company you stood virtually no chance of securing an apprenticeship. But as the saying goes 'there are wheels within wheels'. My mother's cousin was an Amalgamated Engineering Union Official in Crewe who had a quiet word with the 'powers that be' and after a medical at the Works' hospital with the formidable Dr Moors, I was accepted.

My starting position was office boy in the enginemen's department at 48 hours a week for a wage of 12 shillings and 6 pence (62½p). I must say that when I first clapped eyes on my place of work, I was far from impressed. It was a temporary wooden structure, recently repaired because the original had been badly damaged in a German bombing raid. Wreckage was strewn all around the immediate area; bits of twisted metal, shattered railway sleepers and other debris - a dodgy start indeed. Incidentally, from that particular bombing raid, a two foot piece of railway line went straight through the roof of the house of the aunt of my future wife, Kathleen, a street away, landing on the bed. Fortunately, the house was unoccupied at the time.

The function of our office was to organise and run the extensive transport system within the Works itself. The whole company site was impressive in its vastness, stretching virtually from Crewe Station to the west end of the town, approximately a mile and a half in distance and half a mile wide. To put further statistics into perspective, the company employed 20,000 people at its peak (including women in wartime). Sometimes it felt as if the whole town of Crewe worked there. The running side consisted of 17 steam locomotives, each manned by a crew of two, a driver and a fireman. Every loco was also accompanied by a shunter, who coupled and uncoupled the wagons with his shunting pole. He also operated the railway points to direct the wagons through a network of rail lines that led to the various workshops. The wagons contained loads of material and parts, both for general repairs and for the new-build main line locomotives. It was here in this huge network of workshops, seemingly stretching endlessly from Crewe Station, that steam locos were built from scratch - almost every component was made on site virtually down to the last nut and bolt of these wondrous machines.

One of my duties in this complicated system seemed simple enough, although in practice it was anything but. Every Friday I would chase the locos around the site to issue two sweat cloths to every driver and fireman.

The locos were numbered 1 to 17 and were supposed to be in specific areas at certain times - at least that was the theory of it all. This hardly ever turned out to be the case, however. So I would have to run from one place to the next to find them and by the end of the day I would be exhausted and completely worn out. One good thing to come from all the running about, though, was that sometimes you could get a ride on the engine. One driver, Tommy Jones, even let me have a go at driving. He would show me first, the way to ease the regulator lever into position, which allowed steam to enter the pistons. The engine would move forwards, and then by gently adjusting the lever towards the reverse position you would attain the speed required. Tommy's engine had a special duty - it pulled a train of tip-up hoppers filled with tons of molten slag and dross from the steel production plant. The obnoxious load was then taken to a line overlooking a dump. Once there, a tilting mechanism on the hoppers spewed the blazing molten material down a steep slope. The result was what you would call a proper inferno - the noise, the flames, the heat, the smoke and the flying bits of debris tumbling into the air. I saw this many times while cowering on the engine's footplate. To this young boy from the country it was a truly awesome sight.

In general I liked the kind way the drivers treated me, with plenty of brews and sometimes sharing a meal of bacon and eggs cooked on a coal shovel in the boiler fire, also the generous tips I received from them, more than matching my weekly pay.

The steel-making plant (commonly called the "Melts" by the works staff) was a huge corrugated iron building two stories high; the top story housed four massive furnaces. When in operation they roared with the sound of compressed air and ignited powdered anthracite, creating intense heat, melting the pig iron and various minerals to produce the steel. During the process the furnace doors would be opened and the furnace men - protected from the intense heat and glare with leather aprons, gloves and thick black glass face visors - would use long handled shovels to feed in the minerals. The men became soaked in sweat and because of this were allowed a ration of beer each day to compensate for liquid loss.

On my journeys round the departments delivering various bits of paperwork, I would often stop at the "Melts" to watch proceedings. It was fascinating and rather scary to see the molten steel being poured into the moulds producing masses of sparks and flames. The end products were seven-ton ingots of steel.

Being able to wander round the works in my job was a good experience for me but not available to all office boys. The majority of apprentices started directly in the workshops, also as office boys, but were confined to their individual departments with only occasional visits to other shops and to the main general office.

The many departments in Crewe Locomotive Works were the paint shop, wheel shop, steel foundry, iron foundry, brass foundry, brass finishing shop, copper shop, boiler mounting shop, main boiler shop, points and crossing shop, erecting shop, bogie shop, machine shop, machine shop arcade, fitting shop, tender shop, pattern shop, drop stamping shop, smithy, tool room, standards room, case hardening plant, locomotive stores and carriage works. It was a truly massive organisation.

The rest of my time after the weekly engine trips felt quite boring, mostly occupied with filing and delivering documents throughout the works to various shop offices and personnel, including a trip to Crewe Station every morning on my bike with details of traffic movements within the works.

The boss in the department was Mr. Gee, a portly figure and a spitting image of Mr Pickwick. But I had no complaints about him as he was very good to me. Mr Williams, the chief clerk (an ex-soldier) was a dour man who ran the office in military style. The two female staff who assisted him were strictly controlled by finger pointing and nods of the head. Many times he would look round at me sitting behind him and give a sly wink indicating who was in charge!

The area where I worked was called the Old Works and was the site of the first workshops when the railways initially came to Crewe. It contained a boiler shop, signal shop, tin shop, stay shop, joiners shop, millwrights shop, smithy, general stores and the works hospital. It also housed the general offices where all the top management and office staff were based, including the works manager.

Transport for the managers and top brass was provided for visits around the works in a four-wheeled open sided cab. This came under the control of the enginemen's office who also provided the loco. There was a special internal transport system on 18-inch track which conveyed materials and stores between most of the shops and also connected to Crewe station. This was a revolutionary design when set up by the LNWR Locomotive Superintendent John Ramsbottom in 1862.

A famous manager in the late Victorian era was F.W. Webb. Sometimes called the 'King of Crewe' he became the Chief Mechanical Engineer (CME) of the LNWR and revolutionised workshop practice as well as designing many locomotives. He had a great influence on the town of Crewe of which he was twice mayor. He planned the beautiful Queen's Park which was presented to the town by the LNWR and he was also a major benefactor in the Webb Orphanage for the company's employees.

Some other well-known CMEs followed including George Whale and Charles Bowen Cooke but the most famous of all was Sir William Stanier (1932-1944) who designed the "black 5" 4-6-0s, the 8F 2-8-0 freight engines and his record breaking Princess Coronation 4-6-2 No.6220 which achieved a speed of 114mph at Madeley just south of Crewe in 1937.

Many hundreds of homes were built by the railway company in the town centre, forming streets to accommodate its workers. 'Gaffers Row' housed the works foremen, but the big substantial homes were in Delamere Street where the manager and senior engineers resided.

Two churches were built by the railway and the company even provided the town's water and gas supply. The Mechanic's Institute in the town centre housed the company's laboratory and also provided a library, social club and ballroom for the town. A cottage hospital was opened in 1895 once again due to F.W. Webb.

Every conceivable skilled and unskilled trade was employed by the company. All served their apprenticeships within the works, such as boilermakers, platers, coppersmiths, patternmakers, fitters and turners, tinsmiths, blacksmiths, electricians, die sinkers, millwrights and toolmakers. Many more ancillary trades and occupations were taught, such as iron and steel moulding, joinery and carpentry, saddlers working in leather, bricklayers using bricks made on site, painters and signwriters. They even had a fulltime watch and clock repairer who maintained the hundreds of time pieces in the offices and also the pocket watches used by the main line train drivers.

One of the features of the workshop buildings was the black mortar used in the bricklaying. It was made out of crushed slag from the works furnaces - an unusual material replacing sand. This is an example of the many and varied processes that made the site a massive self-contained organisation.

# CHAPTER 3

## Harsh discipline in the machine shop

After six months in the office, I was instructed to report to the main machine shop which was in the area called the Steel Works; this was where the majority of manufactured items were produced. I was told that I would be working in a section that finished, faced and tapped nuts. Millions of them of all sizes; a more boring job could not have been devised. Nut blanks were delivered from the smithy, where they had been stamped and formed out in the hot presses.

I was led by the charge hand to a machine nicknamed the 'War Horse'. To this day I don't know why. I was given 10 minutes instruction on how to start and stop it, how to place the nut in the chuck, how to put the tap in the tap holder, present it to the nut, press the turret handle whereupon the thread was produced. To keep the taps cool, white oil based liquid called 'Bosh' shot from a pipe, not only over the nut but over me; with a bit of adjustment the problem was corrected.

That was my introduction to the final finish of a nut. There were about 20 boys all about my age doing the same as me, but with different size nuts. Some machines had 10 vertical spindles in line, with two boys working like the clappers feeding the nuts into it. But for all the chivvying by those in charge to make sure that the production requirements for the day were met, we had plenty of good moments, such as squirting the cooling liquid at each other, especially if your jet was the most powerful.

As this work was so repetitive and boring, I and the boy who worked on the next machine decided one day to shirk work for the afternoon and take a trip by rail to Chester. On arriving we walked down to the River Dee and hired a rowing boat. We rowed lazily along up the river for a while. Then we turned round and pulled strongly on the oars picking up a good speed and helped along by the current. As we progressed people on the river bank were waving and shouting at us. We thought this was encouragement – but no, the next second the boat tipped forward violently and we were hurled on our backs. We had gone over the weir! The boat was now stuck on the steps but we managed to drag it along the top of the weir to the bank where we could see an irate boatman approaching. We then faced a barrage of abuse before making a shame-faced journey back to the railway station.

Another funny episode I remember vividly: it was a Saturday morning and we were due to finish at 12.30. We were waiting to clock off with our coats on at 12.25, which was forbidden, (no coats on till you clocked off) when someone shouted that the foreman was on his way. Whereupon one of the boys who was wearing a new white sports jacket, whipped it off and threw it under one of the machines where it promptly sank in six inches of cooling fluid.

The foremen (most of whom wore bowler hats) were all powerful. Committing a misdemeanour meant you had an instant reprimand, or in some cases sent home for three days without pay. I was suspended for three days but that will be told later at the time of the event.

When I started there were some rigid working conditions. On weekdays the hours of work were from 8am to 5.45pm, with an hour midday break from 12.30 to 1.30. Saturday was 8 till 12.30 making a total of 48 hours excluding overtime.

No breaks were allowed until either the middle of the morning or middle of the afternoon, which were tea breaks or snacks. You were not allowed to wash your hands. No facilities were provided and hands were cleaned using either turpentine or thin oil and wiped with industrial waste or rags.

Visits to the toilets were the only time you left your machine, note! There was no reading the newspapers in the toilets in those days. Two years prior to my starting work there would be a clerk stationed in every toilet to book people in and out timewise, so as to prevent malingering, (the common name used was 'shit house clerks'). This was discontinued in war time to give clerks a more productive occupation.

One morning a woman approached the brass shop foreman as he was about to enter the Works from the street. She said to him: 'Will you please give my son, Jimmy Hart, this sandwich for his lunch'. The foreman later walked up to the boy, telling him: 'Your mother has sent you a sandwich but if I see you eating it before lunch I will suspend you from work for three days.'

After more than 60 years I still remember the first apprentices I started work with: Don Meredith, Jim Ravenscroft and Roy Townsend (the boy who ruined his coat). I would meet these three boys many times during my working life here.

After six months machine work I was transferred to the fitting shop. This was in the area where connecting rods, internal slide bars, wheels and bogies were repaired. I was to work in the bogie repair section.

Bogies were positioned under the front end of the locomotive and had four small wheels which supported a heavy metal frame. Removed from the loco these are what I was about to help repair. What a change from a comparatively clean environment to a hell hole. That's what it seemed like to me as a 15 year old boy dismantling and handling heavy and filthy black greasy components in a pit.

We worked by candlelight, or oil lamp with smoky white spirit as fuel, with 10 and 50-ton cranes passing on lines overhead and vibrating the ground we stood on. Riveting operations, arc welding and acetylene cutting created an unbearable noise with vivid flashes of light and sparks. Men operated grinding wheels smoothing the rough welded patches, spraying grit and dust in the working area.

As the weeks went by I adjusted somewhat to the work and the dire conditions involved. But because of the handling of heavy components, and the fact that most of the work was performed in cramped spaces with very little room to manoeuvre, it made me very tired at the end on the day.

Something I hated doing at the end of each shift was cleaning the tools which were mostly covered with thick black grease and oil but it was always the apprentices' duty.

The apprentices always worked with time served fitters; these were men who had served a seven year apprenticeship from 14 to 21. The expression "out of his time" at 21 referred to a tradesman fitter. Sometimes the fitter would be lazy, putting all the hard and dirty work on the boy, but in general the standard was good.

All the processes of repair were undertaken in separate sections of the workshops. The fitting shop where the bogies were reconditioned contained four more sections all with different job descriptions. Each section was controlled and run by a leading hand, sometimes called a charge hand. He had a higher rate of pay than the ordinary fitter and would be responsible for production requirements. If satisfactory, he could increase the standard rate of pay with a weekly bonus. A second in command was the first mate; he ordered and had delivered the required materials and parts essential for the repair.

I spent six months in the bogie repair section which was supposed to be the fixed period for each apprentice move. But it did not work in every case because if you were a good worker the charge hand did his best to keep you longer.

My next position was concerned with the refurbishment maintenance and general repair of main line locomotive external and internal motion, mainly spit bearings, which were fitted to the main internal driving wheel journals. Also the connecting rods, which as the name implies were coupled externally to the three sets of wheels. This description is just a simplification. As a boy that was what I was told by my fitter, a very pleasant oldish man to me at the time, but I suppose he could not have been more than 40.

This section was quite different from the previous one and quite clean because the components we received were direct from the cleaning plant. The work involved was not complicated, just replacing worn brass bushes in the connecting rods which were later bored out to fit the external journals. The one operation that required some skill was the white metalled internal journal bearings, which were bedded in by hand using the age old method of scraper and red raddle.(a mixture of red powder and oil)

An incident occurred which strained the relationship between me and Charlie Dickson, my fitter. At the end of the shift when the repair operations were completed, my last duty, apart from cleaning the tools, was to brush down the workbench to remove the dirt and dust that had accrued during the day. When this was completed compressed air was blown over it to complete the cleansing. I was doing the blowing; Charlie was standing to one side, when in an instant the air found its way into a red raddle pot, which was hidden in the well of the bench. Charlie received the full force in the face. His cap, shirt and tie were all dyed red. To say he was slightly annoyed was the misstatement of the century. All hell was let loose! Two other fitters had to dive in and restrain Charlie from killing me. I left the scene hurriedly after offering to wipe his face.

Fortunately it was knocking off time and I went home fearing how he would react the next morning. I met Charlie coming into work, he smiled and said: 'If I had seen that done to someone else I would have laughed my head off'. He was one of the best fitters I worked with and I was sorry when I moved on.

This next department, where I was never to work in again, included the white metalling plant where all axle boxes were re-mettled - the axle box repair section which refurbished all the various types, the wheel turning section and the machining section. There was also a bay where sets were cleaned.

Just to emphasize that it was wartime, hundreds of women were compulsory drafted in. They were called dilutees, which meant that they could work in skilled trades. Most of the lifting cranes were operated by women as were many other tasks, such as machine operatives, centre lathe turners, simple bench work, drilling machines and the fitting of components.

I will say this about the women; they were very hard working and conscientious. They would stand at a machine for hours at a time, never seeming to get bored with the repetition (unlike me). There was quite a bit of opposition in certain trades to women, especially by the coppersmiths who would not allow them to braze or weld. They could fit connections and joints to copper pipes loosely but that was all – they were not permitted to use welding tackle.

My take home pay at this time was less than £2.50 per week after stoppages. The main annual holiday was one week - the first week in July without pay, as were all bank holidays.

I was dreading my next move. I didn't know where it would be. Boys due for a transfer to a new department would be told to report to the shop office where they would be given their clock cards and informed of their new destination. I found out soon enough, which in my case was going to be the worst move possible - the erecting shop.

# CHAPTER 4

## Erecting shop and bogie repair shop

The Erecting Shop was a huge building, bigger than a football field. It contained six belt sections which ran the length of the department. The belts started with a stripping pit where the locos were dismantled, and then to the various first stage sections, where the bare frames of the mainline locomotives were to have the first of their repaired parts fitted along with the frames checked for possible fractures.

Next an intermediate stage where most of the main parts were assembled including the boilers and wheels. Then to a final stage where the whole repair would be completed, ready for the loco to go to the test area for live steam and vacuum brake tests.

When the locos first came in for repair, they were identified as to the type of repair required. Some were heavy repair which was a complete strip down to the bare frame. Intermediate repair was for repair of specific major components. Light repair was mainly for locos that had broken down in traffic, or required a change of wheel sets. And there were many other reasons which could mean admittance to the repair shop. As many as 50 steam locos would be in various stages of repair at any one time in this department. This was as well as a section where new main line locomotives were built.

What I had dreaded was about to happen at this time - a move to the stripping pits which was so well-named because it was the pits. This was where locos were dismantled down to the bare frame; a really filthy black greasy, dusty job. Here were 30 or 40 men and apprentices perched on the boiler and its surrounds taking off the boiler components, others removing the motion parts and pistons, fitters in the pit dropping the wheel set keeps and brake gear and a gang in the driver's cab working to strip off the operating controls, parts and components.

These were the initial steps to prepare for the main dismantling operation, which was the removal of the complete boiler and cab from the frame by crane, then lifting the frame to remove the wheel sets.

At the age of 16, this was where I was to spend my next six months, a horrendous thought at the time. The work was done in dreadful conditions that probably would not be endured these days. Most times when working in the pit with a fitter I would get covered in thick black oil and grease dripping from the underside of the boiler and motion. It was quite dark down there and light only filtered through the slits and cut-outs in the frame, so we used oil lamps for illumination. These were fuelled by white spirit which emitted more black smoke than light.

The most hated job was stripping the smoke box. The parts that had to be removed were held in position by nuts, but these had been worn to mere bits of metal because of the heat and the corrosive effect of the smoke. Consequently, a hammer and chisel were the only way they could be removed. That's when the nightmare began once you started to hammer away, the soot which was about three inches thick covering the surrounding plate work showered down. It got in the eyes, up the nose and breathed in. The coughing and choking were painful, no face masks were available or even in existence. That was just part of the job and no one complained.

At the end of the week, the overalls I wore were absolutely filthy. They were that begrimed they would virtually stand up by themselves. My mother would not touch them, so I would wash them myself. Every Saturday afternoon I would lay them out on the concrete yard at home, pour buckets of water over them, lather with soft soap and scrub with a yard brush. Even after loads of effort they were still stained black in parts. Today detergents would clean them with no effort.

Although the work and conditions were awful, the fitters I worked with were the salt of the earth. These men worked permanently on this section, some of them, for twenty years or more with no chance of a move. But they worked as a happy team, playing jokes on each other, such as lining the brew cans lids with soap. When the steam from the tea hit the lids it melted the soap. You can imagine what the tea tasted like and of course the tainted brew was then thrown over each other amid roars of laughter.

Night shifts were a dread, the whole appearance of the department changed; days had some semblance of light, through the murk of dust and smoke from the riveters' fires and welding operations. But just imagine a gloomy semi-lit dungeon-like workshop, lights a hundred feet up in the roof dimmed by the conditions. Men with tiny oil lamps, straining eyes to see the way to dismantle components and parts safely, the constant noise of hammering echoing from the walls making the ears ache. Tiredness would come quickly around 2 a.m. but you had to carry on working. A favourite trick to overcome the fatigue would be to hold the wrists under the cold water tap for a few minutes and this method worked well.

The noise generated in many of the shops was quite tremendous yet ear muffs were not issued to anyone so it was no surprise that in later years deafness and other hearing problems surfaced.

Thirty years later the company was forced to pay damages to hundreds of workshop staff for hearing loss. Years later I had a test myself by an ear specialist in Manchester which resulted in me receiving a sum of £3,000 for bilateral damage to both ears for the condition of Tinnitus, a continuous ringing and hissing sound in the ear, with no cure.

The ear test I had at that time was in a way quite amusing. The specialist, Dr Lewis, a tiny man, sat me facing him across a desk with a piece of box-like equipment between us. I could just see his eyes peering over the top. He asked me to don the headphones which were connected to the equipment. He then said he would start the process by increasing the sound from zero and would I nod when I started to hear. He looked up at me and asked me if I could hear anything. I said I couldn't so he repeated the question. Three times I told him I couldn't hear a thing. Eventually he leapt to his feet in annoyance: 'You must be able to hear something - it is on full volume!' With that he snatched the headphones from my head and placed them on his own. After a few seconds I could see his expression start to change. He looked up and told me in a strangled voice that the machine was faulty. Anyway, after fiddling about with the box for a while, the test was completed.

One of the fitters I worked with was Joe Dodd. He was a regular night worker, a rough tough man built like a brick outbuilding. He would read the night list which detailed his duties, beckon me to his tool cupboard, pile me with tools and march off to the loco with me staggering along behind. He was a master in the use of a 14 pound big hammer which he would swing with ferocity and rare skill. I would hold the chisel bar against the item which required removing - mostly corroded nuts, while he attacked the end of the bar. It doesn't seem much of a problem except that he was swinging behind me at a bar that was positioned about three inches from my right ear. I've made a mention of the skill involved because I am still here to tell the tale.

Joe was also the recipient of the first electric cable light issued to night workers as an experiment. It had about 50 yards of cable. After being plugged in, Joe wandered round the loco, light in hand, under the frame noting the well illuminated parts to be removed out between the wheels. He then climbed up into the loco cab where he was pulled up short by running out of cable. After a few futile tugs he dumped the light in disgust never to use it again. I as his apprentice then had the job of unravelling all the cable.

Webb 0-6-0 coal engine No. 2153 built in a record 25½ hours in 1878. In WW1 many were sent with the BEF to France. They were extremely reliable and a total of 499 were built. A contemporary comment: "they are probably the simplest and cheapest locos ever made in this country".

Early scene at Crewe North Junction. Main line to North in centre with Chester line to left and Manchester to right. The works were already extensive. c1870

6 wheel tender coupe and ancient 2-2-2 Trevithick 6 foot single loco
FW Webb with Siamese Princes in 1898

Crewe North Junction signal box in 1907 with the "Spider" bridge from
the station to the works with 18 inch gauge line through the middle

Webb 0-8-0 3 cylinder compound No. 1867 newly painted in 1899

Ramsbottom 2-2-2 No.531 "Lady of the Lake" built in 1859. This was the first class of locos to be fitted with a water scoop to pick up water from troughs in the track whilst travelling at speed. Seen with Old Works clock tower.

Ben Robinson was a Crewe Driver who was famous for his exploits for the LNWR in the "Race to the North" in 1895 in competition with the GNR East Coast route. He ran the 141 miles from Crewe to Carlisle with the 2-4-0 "Hardwicke" in 126 minutes at an average speed of 67mph. Seen here in 1900 with the new Webb 4-4-0 No.1926 "La France" which was the 4,000th loco to be built at Crewe.

Webb 2-4-0 Precedent class 482 "Pegasus". Overhaul in No.4 Erecting shop

Webb 0-6-0 Special DX class No.3309 at the Deviation Works with the gardens of management houses in the background

Trevithick 2-2-2 No.3020 "Cornwall" with the Chief Mechanical Engineer's Inspection Saloon at the Deviation Works in 1911

Bowen Cooke George the Fifth class No.2155 "W.C.Brocklehurst" with replica "Rocket" outside Chester Place gardens in 1911

Webb 0-4-0ST Shunter No.3009 built in 1872 and withdrawn in 1946

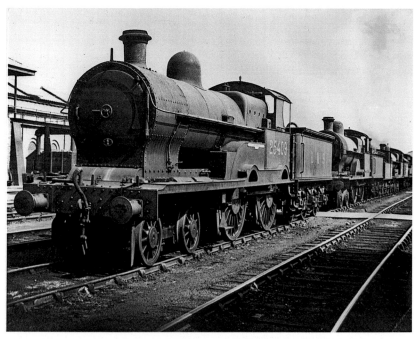

Bowen Cooke 4-4-0 George the Fifth class No.25409 "Dovedale" with Belpaire Firebox

A Royal Visit. King George V arrives in Crewe on 21st April 1913. Appropriately with two 4-4-0 George the Fifth class engines designed by Bowen Cooke, No. 2663 "George the Fifth" and No. 5000 "Coronation" the 5,000th loco to be built at Crewe. Note the gas lamp on latticed pole. Bowen Cooke leads the King below.

No.9 Erecting Shop tidied up for the Royal Visit 1913

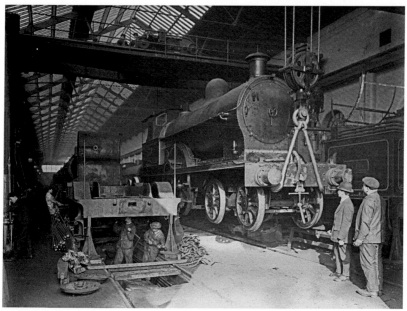

Whale Precursor Class 4-4-0 No. 1312 "Ionic" being lifted in No.9 Erecting Shop.

Boiler Shop on the same day with Hole Punch in right foreground. The boiler on end is probably for George the Fifth class. Note young lad on machine operating lever.

These unique "Cabs" were specially prepared for the royals to travel around the works. The engine is Ramsbottom 0-4-0 tank No.3001 with the guard standing ready at the rear. They were also used by managers/VIPs and to deliver wages.

Armoured train built for WW1 seen in 1915. It consisted of a gun truck and infantry van at each end with the locomotive in the middle with extra water tanks. This was an ex-GNR 0-6-2 tank engine No. 1587. It could be driven from either end and the driver communicated with his fireman by telephone. Note the holes cut in the sides for rifles.

Webb 18 inch gauge loco "Billy" (built in 1875) for the internal tramway system which carried small wagon loads of materials throughout the works and to the railway station. c1920s

Webb improved Precedent 2-4-0 No. 861 "Amazon" freshly painted
with Webb 0-6-2 Coal tank on left

Prince of Wales Class 4-6-0 No. 5683 "Falaba" which was the first engine off
the belt repair system devised by CME HPM Beames in 1927. Mr Beames is
seen with his family, enginemen and works manager and staff

Webb 0-6-0 coal engine No. 8289 inside the Erecting Shop at an early stage of stripping down in 1926

Webb 0-8-0 4 cylinder compound No. 8919 in the Old Works Yard with Crewe North Signalbox at the rear in 1926

41

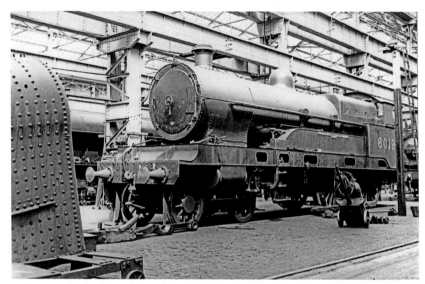

Bowen Cooke Claughton class 4-6-0 No. 6019 "Llewellyn" in the Erecting
Shop for repairs in 1933

Ramsbottom 0-4-0ST Shunter No.1439 built in 1865 and now preserved

Brass Finishing Shop c1930

Erecting Shop No.10 c1930

Erecting Shop working on coupling rods c1930

Boring machine for journal bushes on connecting rod c1930s

Boiler being fitted to frame of Hughes "Crab" 2-6-0  c1930s

Erecting Shop with overhead cranes c1930

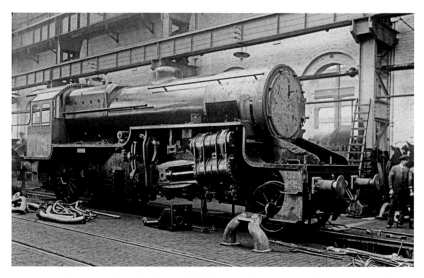

George Hughes "Crab" 5MT 2-6-0 No. 13214 being constructed in 1930 later renumbered by LMS as 2914. These excellent engines worked both passenger and freight trains. 245 were built

Balancing wheels after fitting tyres 1930s

Wheelset repairs c1930s

Mass meeting in Brass Foundry c1920s

Old No4 Erecting shop c1920s

Webb 2-4-2T No.6667 built 1893 withdrawn in 1946

LNWR Mechanics Institute, Crewe town centre c1920s

LNWR Cottage Hospital, Crewe c1920s

Works General Offices, Chester Bridge, Crewe c 1920s
Shows the route of old Chester line before the deviation line was built

Works Manager's House c1920s

Works General Office door and clock built 1876

Tyring wheels c1930s

Wheel Lathe c1930s

Webb 0-4-2 Crane Tank engine No.3248 was built in 1894
It was used for shunting and lifting jobs around the works with
a lift capacity of 3 tons.  c1935

Building the experimental "Turbomotive" 4-6-2 No. 6202 "Princess Anne" in 1933. It was later involved in the Harrow disaster in 1952.

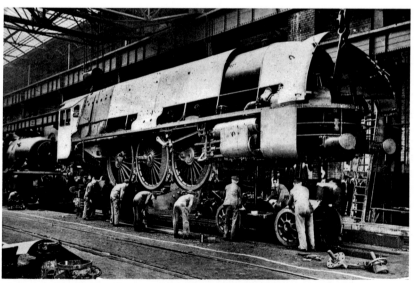

Fitting bogie on new Stanier Coronation Class loco c1937

Three new Coronation Class 4-6-2 Pacifics outside the Paint Shop in 1937:
6220 "Coronation", 6221 "Queen Elizabeth" and 6222 "Queen Mary"
These first streamlined locos were painted in blue and silver and were designed
by Sir William Stanier to run on the "Coronation Scot" express between Euston
and Glasgow. Crewe Driver Tom Clarke set a speed record of 114mph in 1937
with 6220 at Madeley just south of Crewe on a special press run.

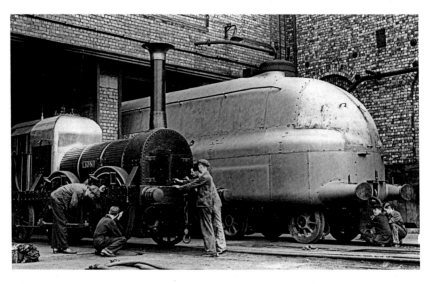

Newly built  Coronation Class No.6229 "Duchess of Hamilton" in workshop
grey in 1938. Seen with 0-4-2 "Lion" built in 1837 for the Liverpool &
Manchester Railway which had been overhauled for the London &
Birmingham Railway centenary

43323 Johnson Class 3F 0-6-0 (built 1892) taking water
outside the Signal Shop c1950s

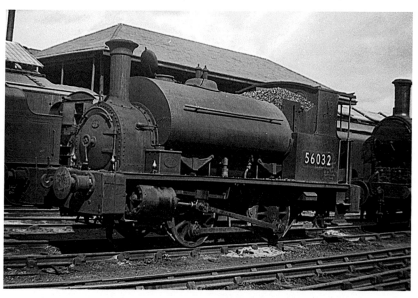

56032 Drummond Caledonian 0-4-0ST "Pug" Works shunter
built 1900 and withdrawn 1960

52464 Aspinall L&Y 3F 0-6-0 (built 1917) The most numerous class on the L&Y with 448 built. c1950s. This engine worked on Crewe works and was withdrawn in 1961

49117 Bowen Cooke Class 7F 0-8-0 (built 1910 and rebuilt in 1943) c1950s

47865 Webb 0-4-2T saddle tank (built 1901) used as works shunter until 1953

44765 "Black Five" 4-6-0 with Caprotti Valve gear and double chimney. c1950

58902 Webb 0-6-2 Coal tank (built 1884) c1950. She had a very long life before being withdrawn in 1954

49151 Bowen Cooke Class 7F 0-8-0 and 45593 Jubilee Class 4-6-0 "Kolhapur" (now preserved) outside the Loco Stores in 1950

Locos under repair in Erecting shop in 1953 including 46257 (2nd from right) Coronation Class 4-6-2 "City of Salford"

View of Crewe Works in 1957 from Crewe North Shed showing the works entrance and original buildings. Class 5 4-6-0 45289 and Royal Scot 4-6-0 46125 "3rd Carabinier" prepare to move off shed

46443 Ivatt Class 2MT 2-6-0 repairs c1960s

BR 9F 2-10-0 Nos. 92016/77 repairs c1960s

Diesel engine piston assembly

Diesel engine assembly

61

Diesel engine repair shop

Bryan Skellon (second from left) with apprentice friends

Bryan as Works Inspector testing an electric pantograph

# CHAPTER 5

## Dangerous working during World War 2

It was with a sense of great relief when I departed from the stripping pits area, away from all that dirt and grime. I was told to report to Mr Hasledine, the charge hand on the first stage. He looked me up and down wondering if this tall skinny lad would be of any use in the heavy work involved. He took me to a fitter, who had just poked his head out of the pit, (the pits were three feet six deep, four feet wide and the loco frames sat on stands over the pit).

Doug the fitter was a little man who when it came to lifting put all the weight on me, but he looked after me in many ways. He was a skilful tradesman, showing me the correct way to use tools, except for the day when he was driving a long bolt into the frame with me holding it. He missed and flattened my little finger; the scars are there to this day.

Many times when handling rough castings or newly machined components that had not had the burrs trimmed you could receive some quite serious cuts.

Another danger was damage to the eyes from grinding machine particles. I had a piece of steel in the eye, which the company doctor, Dr Moores, an unfeeling man, removed with what I felt was a six inch nail - it was so painful.

A funny incident which I observed was a man grinding an axle box weld. He was wearing a face mask,(the only men issued with them) in which he had poked a hole to accommodate a cigarette he was puffing. He was breathing a good healthy mixture of smoke and dust.

You could also be temporarily blinded by the flash from electric welding operations. You would be in agony with the feeling of intense prickling pain; it meant a visit to the medical centre where the nurse would administer eye drops. It would take many hours before the pain subsided and the sight became normal.

I saw some terrible injuries while working in this department. A five hundredweight casting slid off a two wheeled cart, which over balanced. The man behind pushing it fell forward; the casting landed on his head and killed him instantly. Another time, a fitter had the arteries in his arm sliced open when a steel plate being lifted by an overhead crane fell on him; he was off work for six months.

Men and boys who suffered injuries at work received no compensation, only sick pay. Claiming for trauma, stress and loss of earnings, as applied to modern industry had not even been thought about.

The fact that the first four years of my working life were spent in the period of World War Two made conditions different from normal. From the age of sixteen you were obliged to work overtime, which could mean eight till eight six days a week and a night shift from eight in the evening till eight in the morning. From 18 years of age it was twelve hours shifts, seven days per week, nights and days. Shifts were changed so personnel worked fortnights about.

The men who worked days had to spend one full night a week on fire watch duty in the Works. So, although the men worked in a reserved occupation, which meant that they were exempt from military service, the hours spent away from home was not an easy option.

Another sign of a wartime situation was the sight of military tanks being assembled and tested in the Works. There were also dozens of German prisoners of war, many from the 'U' boat German submarines. They arrived every morning with an armed escort from Crewe Hall which was a prisoner of war camp. Most of these prisoners were quite arrogant, especially a tall red bearded individual who had been a U-boat Captain. He and others had to be chivvied to carry on with their work, which was removing the thick dried grease and oil from the Workshop floor.

There was also a Works Home Guard System. Men who were volunteers were issued with uniforms, tin hats and revolvers. A different team patrolled the Works each night; again it was a 12-hour stint above the normal day shift.

The following tale is a perfectly true one: A Sergeant who shall be nameless, an ex-professional boxer, was drilling his men in the art of self-defence, when he decided to prove that tin helmets were capable of preventing head injury. Armed with a service revolver, he instructed one of his men to don his tin helmet. He then rained a vicious blow on the hat with the butt of the gun where-by the man collapsed unconscious to the floor. What was not obvious before the blow was struck was that the man had removed the webbing from inside the helmet - the cushion keeping the tin away from the head. This episode travelled round the Works causing much merriment, but the man involved was not amused. He spent a week off work with concussion.

My next job was to the second stage of a loco's construction where the frame was fitted with the main equipment and components, the boiler, cab, cylinders, pistons and slide bars, as well as ancillary bits and pieces. The mates I worked with were good. We had plenty of fun together although the work was heavy and constant; the charge hand regularly patrolled the section to make sure that everyone was occupied with their specific task.

The fitter I worked with had done the same job for years; the assembly of cock gear, which in simple terms allows a surplus amount of exhaust steam to escape from the cylinders. All around the cylinders where the cock gear was fitted was a layer of white asbestos, three inches thick. Large pieces of this were displaced during the fitting process. It was picked up and thrown about like snowballs. As well as the cylinder insulation, blue asbestos jackets were wrapped around the whole boiler - little did we know of the dangers.

It was not until many years later that asbestos of both kinds, blue and white, led to the death of dozens of Crewe Works staff from asbestosis. Men were still losing their lives sixty years later.

The wheeling of the part-finished loco was carried out on this section. Two 50-ton cranes were required, one at each end of the frame. Massive hooks would be secured under the buffer beams and the frame would rise slowly. When sufficient height was reached, the three sets of wheels would be rolled manually into position under the relevant horn blocks (the axle box location) and the cranes would then lower the frame with fitters standing in the pit guiding the axle boxes down into position. The connecting rods, some of which weighed at least a ton, would then be lifted manually by a team of men and secured to the wheels.

All the while these activities were going on other repair functions were being carried out by other trades, such as riveting, drilling, plating, welding (both gas and electric). These areas were a hive of industry at all times, excessively noisy, hazy with dust and the stench of fumes from various processes and activities.

By this time snacks and a brew were allowed in mid-morning - 10 minutes to make the tea and to eat the sandwiches. Woe betide anyone who overdid this 10-minute rule as the foremen patrolled their departments assiduously.

Each section had its own tea trolley where you could buy tea, cakes and sandwiches. A canteen lady was in charge and some of them arrived with their trolleys earlier than others. One day, keen to take advantage of an early brew, I strolled over to another section and joined their queue.

Arriving at the trolley, the lady looked me up and down and told me she wouldn't serve me because I wasn't from her section. To my dying shame I came out with an expletive - just common Workshop language, but not apparently common to this lady. With that she departed, leaving the trolley where it stood with about 20 men in the queue deprived of a brew.

I went back to my workplace, hoping my outburst would lead to nothing, but she had gone straight to the department's superintendent to report me for using bad language. I was subsequently sent for by the 'big boss' Mr Bird.

Apprehensively I climbed the stairs to his office and before I could knock a voice bellowed at me to enter. He sat hunched in a chair, all 20 stone of him, an intimidating sight. 'Skellon', he said, 'you have used bad language to one of my tea ladies, you will now go and apologise to her. If she accepts your apology you will not be suspended. If not you will be sent home without pay for three days.' I duly went up to the woman and apologised. But I can tell you, she was no lady, because all she did was laugh, as did her workmates. I was relieved, however, that nothing more came of the incident.

Working nights, fortnights about on this section, was a strange existence. From my regular nightly sleeping habits to starting work at eight o'clock in the evening was strange. After a normal sleep on Sunday night, up all day Monday, then starting work on a twelve hour shift from eight till eight it was twenty four hours awake. By the time the shift ended I was absolutely drained of energy. Tuesday's sleep was long and solid, as was the rest of the week.

Although the work was hard and tiring, some of us entertained ourselves during the hour-long dinner breaks by playing cards, mostly for pennies. The arguments, the banter and the ribald comments during these games created entertainment for those not even playing.

For those with plenty of energy during the dinner break, a game of so-called football was played in a wide open space where locos were traversed about during the day, but was clear at night. The ball was made of sweat cloths and industrial hand wipes tied up with string. Men would come from other sections to play. Two motley teams would be formed and then the fun would start.

What made things rather difficult were the raised railway lines which ran the length of the playing area. The mob (which is the only way to describe the two teams) would chase the ball from end to end; men and boys were knocked sprawling or flying full length after tripping on the rails. During the time I worked in the area no one was seriously hurt, however. But plenty of them finished the match limping even if they were in the fray again the next night - men as tough as old boots.

After arriving for duty at night, the first mate would read out the work list for each fitter and apprentice as compiled by the charge hand from the day shift. This indicated the work to be completed by morning. It was, therefore, in every man's interest to finish the work as quickly as possible in the hope that a spare hour or so could be spent taking a quick nap.

Sleeping on nights was a punishable offence, as you can imagine in a regime like that, so any sleeping places had to be hideaways - anywhere the foremen would not think of looking. So one of the best places was in the loco fire box or footplate. One of the favourite places, which was to have serious consequences in later years (as I have mentioned before) was in the blue asbestos lagging store. Men would virtually wrap themselves in this material and sleep, unknowingly risking their lives with the inhalation of asbestos fibres.

An episode that caused some concern and ribald comments in the department was the award of a wartime medal (I think a B.E.M.) to a leading hand, for devotion to duty. He controlled about 15 men, who worked 12 hours a day, seven days a week while he sat at a desk all day wearing the seat of his trousers out. The explanation for this award from the management was that he got the medal as a representative of his men.

All-in-all, though, I had some good times in this department, the camaraderie and friendliness of the mates was the best. They would laugh and joke no matter what the conditions of work, dirty or hard, and they would help you without question. Anyone having their first look at the majority of them would think they were a motley mixture; filthy overalls, an assortment of belts, leather, rope and string, quite a few moustaches and beards. They worked hard and played hard, the latter noticeable by the morning-after-the-night-before headaches that were often in evidence.

# CHAPTER 6

## More dangers in the Tender Shop and Iron Foundry

My next move at 17 was to the Tender Shop where all main line locomotive tenders were repaired. This work was also very dirty, not only with grease and oil but contaminated with stagnant water and lime and coal deposits.

Tenders were used to carry coal as fuel and also water to supply the loco boilers. The fireman shovelled coal into the loco firebox, but the water supply was pressurised through injector steam valves into the boilers. This is a very simple explanation, but obviously there is much more to it than that. The tender was normally filled with water via its top at depots and stations. But on many main lines, to avoid stopping, the water was drawn into the tenders at speed from water troughs between the railway lines by a pick-up chute which was lowered by the fireman at specific places on the loco's route.

To affect a repair, say of the inlet valves, the procedure was an absolute nightmare. First, to gain access to the water tanks, I had to squeeze through a hole on top of the tender just 14 inches wide, then climb down a seven foot ladder into the base of the tank. I would descend into this jet black hole with only a lighted candle in my hand, to land in a three or four inch thick 'carpet' of white lime-coloured mud.

Now the route to the inlet valves was at the farthest end of the tank some 12 feet away. To reach them I would have to crawl on my hands and knees, through cut-out baffle plates to begin dismantling them. Then you would find that the securing nuts and threads of the bolts holding hem in place would be corroded with hard lime deposits, so this had to be chipped away first and, most times, the nuts would have to be split using a hammer and chisel.

You can imagine the thoughts of a young boy, especially when the candle was accidentally knocked over plunging the whole area into pitch black darkness. Then the struggle began to find the matches deep in the overall pockets - with thick muddy hands. Don't think I am over exaggerating the conditions - there was worse to come. Within this stew of mud were crawling creatures, frogs, tadpoles, leeches, newts, water beetles, snails and on rare occasions small grass snakes. This array of wildlife would have been picked up from the water troughs between the lines. To cap all of this, the platers on the outside of the tender would start riveting patches on the worn areas of the tender making the noise inside magnified into an horrendous din…you can understand me feeling sorry for myself having to contend with that lot!

After the top portion of any repair, the frame and wheels would come next. With all the water flying about underneath a tender, erosion was rife; every nut, bolt and pin would be thick with rust. This was when the big hammer and chisel came into use and in some cases oxygen and acetylene cutters.

All apprentices were allowed to use the cutters - but without specific training; this led to some hairy situations when the cylinders became dangerously overheated. Then it was every man for himself, except for a few brave souls who would douse the cylinders with buckets of water to cool them.

One of the apprentices I worked with was called Donald, who, to say the least, was a bit odd and there never seemed to be a dull moment when he was around. He was interested in explosives, probably due to the fact that it was wartime. One day, he approached me with the idea of making an explosive device. Quite simply it comprised a metal nut with the bolt just entering the thread, the open end of the nut filled with a sulphur powder mixture and then another bolt screwed tightly to compress the powder. So this is what we constructed.

With our device loaded, we walked to the outside path whereupon Donald suddenly hurled it in mid-air with no thought of danger to us or anyone else. At the end of its flight it hit a corrugated iron fence bounced off it and hit a man in the middle of his back. The man fell forward with a scream. Donald and I shot back quickly into the Workshop feigning innocence. The sequel was that the man was shocked but not physically hurt. We heard afterwards that he thought something had fallen off the roof and landed on him. Later, Donald surreptitiously recovered the missile from a drain where it had lodged.

One morning, Donald, came into work with signs of a beating - he had bruises everywhere. He explained that he had picked up a mortar bomb after watching a military exercise between the Crewe Fire Service and men of the Cambridgeshire Regiment, (later to be captured and made prisoners of war by the Japanese) who were stationed at Crewe Hall.

The exercise had become quite serious because the Fire Service men started spraying the soldiers with jets of water from their hose reels. The soldiers then retaliated, driving over the hoses and shredding them with the tracks of their Bren Gun Carriers which resembled a small tank.

Donald took the mortar bomb home and showed it to his dad, who explained with a little knowledge, that it contained a time fuse, which could delay the explosion when the bomb was fired at a target. The thoughts, which went through Donald's head at this explanation makes the mind boggle. He told me he took the mortar into the greenhouse - his dad's pride and joy - clamped it in a vice and turned the time fuse with a hammer and chisel.

Nothing happened, so he was just about to give it another go when his mother called him into the house for his dinner. Everyone had just sat down when an almighty explosion rent the air. As well as shaking the house and the plates on the table, the greenhouse was blown to bits. After Donald had related this latest explosive incident, I could see by his bruises that his dad had not been very happy with him at the outcome to his little experiment.

Talking of bombs and explosions, quite a few tenders that came for repair were built in America and had been rescued from the sea bottom after the ships transporting them had been bombed in English ports. These were the most difficult to repair as they were encrusted with rust and filled with debris and this meant a complete overhaul.

Apart from the tenders, many locomotives suffered great damage through enemy bombing. One I saw had a length of railway line protruding from it. The line had pierced the smoke box at the front end, passed straight through the boiler and ended with about three foot of rail sticking out at the back of the tender - such was the force of the explosion.

While I have already mentioned Donald, many of the mates I worked with were rare characters. One named Big Les would carry a huge bag of tools atop the tender. When he had finished the job, he would then throw the tools overboard irrespective of who was working underneath. Everyone who was about to work in the same area would reconnoitre to see where Les was situated.

My uncle Frank worked close-by as a gas welder. A big bluff man with a very broad Cheshire dialect: 'ow art tha' going on youth' he would say to me as we met. Although he had his leg pulled about his speech he never took offence. He was a mild man, but knowing his First World War record as a Lead Horseman of a field gun, in the front line in France where he was wounded, I knew he was also a tough man.

One of the worst accidents I have encountered was in this department. The main chemical used in the cleaning plant's tanks to remove oil and grease was liquid caustic soda. It was stored before being used in 50-gallon steel barrels. The plant operator was required to top-up the tanks to the correct level but, this day, had trouble removing the screwed outlet cap from the barrel with the normal tool, so he asked a young fitter named Broomfield if he could unscrew it with a hammer and chisel.

The barrel had been standing outside most of the morning, in the blazing hot sun. These conditions had allowed the liquid to pressurise the barrel, which was to result in an awful tragedy. Partway through the release of the cap the caustic soda sprayed with extreme force directly into the eyes of the fitter. He reacted after shouting out in agony by trying to find a water tap to wash out the chemical from his eyes. But although being rushed to a tap by his workmates who had observed what had happened - it was too late and, tragically, he lost the sight of both eyes.

That was, of course, a terrible thing to have happened but other experiences were funny - that is if you have a warped mind like me. One that was amusing was when Fred, a labourer who worked on our section, decided that because of wartime fuel rationing he would keep his home fires burning by helping himself to a supply from one of the tenders which was loaded with egg-shaped compressed coal dust pellets (a wartime product). He proceeded to tie the bottoms of his overall legs with string then fill them with the fuel pellets.

The exit from the Works to the street was up a long slope. Fred was forcing his way up the incline with his still loaded legs when the string came adrift and the fuel pellets cascaded down behind him. I was told by the men who saw this that he did not alter his gait, or his expression but just carried on, knowing that if the gatekeeper who had heard the shouts of laughter had actually spotted the fuel leak he would have been in serious trouble.

The dinner break when working nights lasted an hour. If you were dog tired, (especially when you had been up all day Monday), it was a time when almost everyone would take a nap. During the winter months the shop was heated by 'Bee Hive' stoves (named after their shape). These had chimneys going through the roof above, and only gave out a reasonable amount of heat if you stood virtually on top of them - so we would sleep as close as possible.

One night, I and six others were fast asleep when we were awakened by an almighty explosion; some joker had dropped an explosive fog signal in the fire. These were a two inch diameter half an inch thick metal case filled with an explosive powder. In normal use these were used to warn the loco drivers, especially in the vicinity of signals during thick fog, (they were placed on the line and exploded by the wheels of the loco).

The noise was not the only problem. Years-old thick layers of soot and ash from the 30-feet chimney buried us. We were as black as coal with eyes and noses full of ash, soot and dust. It was treated as a great joke among the day shift workers but we were not amused.

Although the working conditions were pretty grim in the Tender Shop, they were not half as bad as the department next door, the Iron Foundry. Even looking through the intervening door was depressing. The whole area was shrouded by thick dust caused by the continuous knocking out of burnt sand from the fired moulds. This coupled with the heat and glare from the pouring of molten iron into the prepared moulds made working barely tolerable.

The incidence of chest problems was common, with many men in later life suffering from silicosis. Remember there was no redress from the company regarding compensation in those days.

There was a serious incident in the foundry, when a man lost his life through sheer negligence. His job was to blast the sand out of freshly cast loco cylinders with a high pressure water hose. He was provided with an air tight rubber suit and adjoining helmet which was fed fresh air by way of a pump. The lubrication for the pump was a special oil which could be ingested or breathed in with no harm to health.

Unbeknown to him the pump's lubrication system had been inadvertently filled with ordinary engine oil. This, mixed with air by the pumps action, was inhaled by the man over a period of several weeks until he suddenly collapsed and died. A post mortem found that his lungs were black and that the cause of death was due to the use of incorrect oil - but no one was blamed.

Many men travelled to work by bus. This was normally at 7.30 in the morning. These buses were single decked, with a central hand rail and seats down each side. They held 60 passengers, mostly standing, and packed like sardines. The men called them cattle trucks. The fare from the end of Waldron's Lane where I lived was a penny and half in old money. More often than not I would miss the bus and then the old bike would be used to transport me to work.

Crewe Works fitters and turners and other workmen were represented by the Amalgamated Engineering Union. Membership was compulsory, even for apprentices as young as 16. As I was a lifelong Conservative (then at the age approaching 18) I objected to this so I would delay my subs deliberately.

After a few weeks a letter would arrive from the number seven union branch informing me that I owed a certain amount, and if I did not keep up to date I could be expelled from the union, with the result that I would not be represented in any dispute with the management (in peace time I would have lost my job).

On one particular occasion I was called to the branch to explain the persistent delay in paying my subs. Turning up at the venue, a church annex in the town, I entered the room to be met by about 10 men seated at a long table - a kangaroo court.

The branch chairman, Brother Thomas, started to give me a lecture on the benefits of being a member of the union. He said one of the things that would be available to me in future years was that the union could finance me if I ever desired to become a member of parliament. I replied in all innocence that should that happen, then I would like to be a Conservative MP. My remark caused uproar, and shouts of 'no' with several of them banging their hands on the table. I was dismissed promptly with a warning to pay up on time - but I never did.

Unions can be useful in many instances, but when it comes to restrictive practices as was the case many times in Crewe Works, it could cause disruption and loss of work contracts. I can say that I never went on strike, although on two or three occasions strikes were ordered by the unions. My non-strike resolve was helped due to the fact that I could arrange to attend training courses, mostly at the training centre in Derby, away from what I regarded as the self-important destructive actions of shop stewards.

The mode of dress in the Works was standard, particularly for the foremen. All of them without exception wore blue serge suits with tie and white shirt, black shoes, and to cap it all, as the saying goes, a black bowler hat.

One great thing about the dress was that you could see them coming a mile off. When a foreman was off sick or on holiday, the senior leading hand or a department inspector would deputise. From wearing brown smocks the previous day, they would appear in (guess what) blue serge suits with tie and white shirt, black shoes and bowler hat.

Good time keeping was strictly observed. The rule for all workshop staff was that for every minute you were late, five minutes pay was deducted. Each man and boy had a clock card with a unique number. He would insert the card into the slot within the clock and press a lever. The time would then be printed in the correct section of the card. This happened four times a day; on entering in the morning, leaving and starting at midday break, and at the end of the working day.

The punishment for clocking misdemeanours was severe; late five times a week could mean a three day suspension from work without pay. Clocking other people on or off invariably meant the sack. The punishment meted out led to some ingenious schemes of clock manipulation. The cards were collected and checked each week so it allowed a timespan of correction.

If people were late, a piece of paper would be stuck to the card in the correct space just allowing, for example, the eight o'clock sign to be printed excluding the minutes, the following day the reverse would happen with the hour being covered, then by bending the card at the bottom or forcing it further into the slot, the previous day's correct time could be entered.

Just outside this department was the works canteen where midday meals could be bought and eaten, sitting on long rows of wooden benches. It was a place very sparse and bare. Workers' Playtime concerts given by entertainers would be performed about once a fortnight to boost our morale. The thing which sticks in my mind the most was the occasional sale of a chocolate biscuit called 'Wagon Wheels'. It was about four inches in diameter and as hard as a brick and covered in what was described as chocolate. Men and boys would queue for them because anything sweet was a rare luxury in wartime (I believe they are still made today).

# CHAPTER 7

## Stay shop and my suspension

My next move was a couple of months overdue, but the charge hand I worked for said he was reluctant to let me go. This was because I more than satisfied him work-wise. As I have mentioned before, they could hold on to you if they thought fit. I had become quite concerned in one case as one of his apprentices had been with him for two years, and quite possibly this youth could remain on the job to the age of 21 and become a fitter with a permanent position. After working in the conditions described there was no way I would stay.

After describing my position to the shop foreman and getting little response, I explained my problem by letter to the person controlling the movement of apprentices, Mr O'Neal, who was the under manager. Things moved quickly from then on and my next move was to be the Stay Shop.

Stay Shop Old Works, just a stone's throw away from my old place of employment, the Works Enginemen's Office also took me back to operating machinery. The Stay Shop as the name implies produced metal and copper stays used in the manufacture of locomotive boilers. It was nothing special - just a straight piece of metal, six inches in length, three quarters of an inch in diameter, undercut in the middle and threaded both ends. The total per shift was 120 - that is what made the work so boring.

The machines were turret lathes, belt driven from overhead main shafting which made the work place extremely noisy, but this was no big problem when pitted against the disadvantages of other workshops.

Although a set number of stays had to be produced each day (and counted at the end of the shift by a checker) it allowed very little rest time. The practice was to make a few extra and hide them, saving them to make up your total when on nights; this method enabled you to finish work in less time, enabling you to hide away for a bit of a nap.

Although you might think that there would not be much danger working in a fixed position, you would be mistaken. The waste cuttings from the turning operation were razor sharp and many deep and serious cuts were sustained.

One of the worst happened to my sister Joyce. When the war started Joyce along with other women were drafted into the Works. (By the time I arrived in this shop late in 1945, the women had been transferred to other jobs or allowed to resume their peace time occupation).

Joyce had left her lathe to make a cup of tea in the morning break when she walked into a razor-sharp cutting stretched between the legs of a machine. This sliced apart the sinews in front of her ankle causing her foot to drop - a very serious injury. She was taken to the nearby company hospital but the injury was too complicated to be treated there so she was sent off to the Manchester Royal Infirmary. Joyce was off work for three months, given only meagre sick pay and not a penny compensation. The unsightly scars remained with her all her life.

On another occasion the apprentice who worked on the next lathe to me was using a file to remove a burr from a stay (a practice that was against all safety regulations) when his overall sleeve became caught in the revolving component. I didn't hear him shout at first due to the general noise, but I certainly heard his screams as he was dragged closer into the machine.

I ran over to him and just in time stopped the machine. At that instant he was about to be dragged off his feet by the pull on his overalls. He was very lucky to have escaped serious injury or even death. As it was he had deep cuts on his wrists. The thought of it at the time really shook me but the apprentice was shaking like a leaf for a long time afterwards.

It was not all doom and gloom, though. We had some relatively happy times especially on nights, if you can call crazy things amusing. One event that caused merriment among the boys and apoplexy to management was the case of a repaired boiler positioned on a trolley awaiting transport. Someone tied a rope around its dome (a large projection on top of the boiler) and lashed the other end to a wheel on the trolley. When it started to be towed from its position in a narrow tunnel, the rope tipped the boiler over and it became trapped. It took two days to extract it. After intense interrogation by the foreman, the men who had been working that night in the vicinity denied all knowledge of the incident. Blame could not be determined or punishment meted out, simply because 100 staff were too many to suspend. I can say now that I may have been one of the culprits of the prank.

Now to explain when I did come to suffer a suspension: when being transferred from one department to the next, one's issue of clean overalls did not travel with you and it was sometimes several weeks before they caught up with you. To ensure a weekly change in the meantime, a chit was issued to enable you to pass security outside the main offices to your previous place of work to make the change.

My mistake, without a pass, was to attempt a sneaky trip by crawling bent double, supposedly out of sight of security, along a wall. But I had been spotted before my contortions began by a security man who, unbeknown to me, had appeared from a side door behind me. I was apprehended and asked for my name and number and told to report back to my shop foreman who informed me that I would be recommended for suspension for leaving my point of work without permission.

And so, a fortnight later, on a Tuesday night shift at about midnight, I was told to report to the shop office. The only people there were the shop foreman, a Mr Bates and his wife (who could not keep a straight face). He read me the Riot Act as if my absence from my work was a major crime and presented me with a management letter suspending me from work for three days without pay, beginning on the following Monday.

I found out later that Mr Bates had been attending Crewe Theatre and had made a special journey to issue me with the reprimand - it was that important.

To snatch half an hours sleep on nights was not always possible because of the difficulty in finding the time and also a decent place to hide as I have stated previously. Although we might have achieved our nightly target well before the end of the shift, you were not allowed to sleep, but expected to hang around your machine till knocking off time. The foremen seemed to know many of the sleeping spots, but the favourite and most ingenious one which was never found while I worked there was in the next department, the Boiler Shop and was located behind a row of furnaces.

The bed lay on top of a mains water pipe, a gas pipe and pressurized air pipes, which with a few boards and bags added was reasonably comfortable except for the noise and vibration. The beat and sound of the huge compressors which supplied the air to the furnaces made the pipes lift every few seconds and while this might have driven some to sleep, I never got a wink.

A frightening event which happened here concerned a young fitter. In the middle of a deep sleep he was awakened by an enormous bang and vibration which virtually threw him off the bed.

He found out the next day that the Rolls Royce factory had been bombed by a German aircraft and the bomb had hit the water main in the factory. It was certainly a frightening experience for him but nothing like the tragedy for the 17 Rolls Royce workers who were killed in that air raid.

Around and over the shop door was a tarpaulin-covered draught excluder. The top made a very comfortable bed, about six feet square. On this particular morning there was a visit to the shop by the Works Manager. As he and his assistants walked through the door a head appeared. It was the bed's inhabitant awaking from his slumber at nine o'clock - an hour after his normal finishing time. He was ordered down and given a good telling off which included a week at home without pay.

The machining process within this department was simple, but the daily quantity of metal stays that had to be produced by each operative was very hard to achieve. At the end of the shift the total number from each machine was counted by a checker and placed in a locked compound. The number related to the amount of bonus you would receive with your standard weekly pay.

Due to the ingenuity of hard-done-by staff, a way was found to supplement this quantity when working on the night shift. No picking the lock on the compound gate or making a hole in the wire fence - we just had to climb on to an adjacent stationary boiler and drop down inside the compound where you could then help yourself to the amount required for your time.

This practice continued for a considerable time and well after I left the department. But as all good things must come to an end, the purloining of metal stays from the compound was discovered, evident by the vast decrease of stock. Due to increased security and with the fitting of a metal roof to the compound, the good times for the boys then ended.

# CHAPTER 8

## Brass finishing shop and a death by cyanide

My period in the Stay Shop was now at an end. I was told to report to the Brass Finishing Shop which would be the department in which I would spend the longest part of my working life when my apprenticeship ended. After reporting to the shop office, I was escorted to Freddy Hinton the charge hand who ran a machining section. He was a very untidy man sporting a walrus moustache and was nearing retirement which showed by the chaotic way he organised the work.

The metal cabin offices, where all charge hands operated from were mostly models of efficiency, but Freddy's was littered with paperwork. He would delve through the piles when sorting out your next machining operation. Many times I set the machine up to start when he would saunter up with another type of job more urgent. He never lost the authority of his position - I mean, he made sure that everyone contributed fully to the bonus target.

The machine I was to operate was manufactured by a German firm called 'Pittler'. It was a horizontal turret lathe of very unusual design, the only one of its kind in the Works. It seemed a strange irony that during the war with Germany, I would be operating a machine made by the enemy.

The work involved in this department was mainly the manufacture and repair of all brass components used in a railway locomotive. They consisted of items used to convey and expel water to and from the boilers, injectors and ejectors, brass connections, Yorkshire couplings, drivers' steam and vacuum brake valves, pressure gauges, brass nuts and tail pipes, plus many more brass and phosphor bronze items.

The machines which produced the manufactured parts were many and various such as capstan and turret lathes, centre lathes, boring machines, drills, slotters and planers.

One of the big advantages with the shop was the relative cleanliness. Most of the machining was performed without the use of oil or coolant. Brass generates little heat when being formed with a machine tool and although a dust was produced, which looked like gold dust in electric light and sunlight, it was not considered a danger to health, although there was no proof of that.

This was not the case with many other processes which were carried out in the department. The most dangerous was the plating plant used to copper plate the lead inserts in boiler fusible tapered plugs. It consisted of two vats containing a cyanide/water mixture. Suspended in this were copper ingots together with the plugs, charged in sequence with a low live and neutral voltage which, due to the electrical agitation, copper particles became attracted to the lead to form a thin copper non corrosive barrier. The plugs were fitted into loco boilers' water jackets as a safety device. If for some reason the boiler lost its water the lead would melt with the heat thus relieving the boiler pressure. This description may seem long winded but is necessary to convey the reason for the use of a deadly poisonous chemical.

Each month the plant's operator would change the mixture by emptying it down the main drains - probably killing off bacteria over a range of 20 miles. He would then walk to an unlocked store where the cyanide powder - compressed into egg shapes - was kept in an open cardboard box. He would pile the eggs in a scoop by hand and walk back to the plant. Many times I saw powder from the eggs spilling to the floor as he walked past my machine. Apart from this dangerous practice, the plant was used by the night shift as a dinner site and lunch boxes would be placed on the surrounding edges of the vats together with the cups and brew cans.

They say that ignorance breeds contempt and this was a classic case. No one realised the dangers especially when management paid no attention to the safety aspect until the following incident which led to fatal consequences.

It was a well-known fact by fishermen that when cyanide liquid drops were added to a piece of cloth outside the entrance to a wasps' nest, the resulting cyanide gas would kill the occupants. The wasp cake could then be dug out of the nest and the larva used for bait.

A worker from the next shop used a bottle with a tapered stopper to provide him with enough cyanide liquid to use on a fishing trip to the River Severn at Shrewsbury. He had told his mates about a nest that he had discovered there on a previous visit. He said he was going to take it, by which he meant removing the cake and using it for bait. He went on the trip the following Saturday afternoon but was found dead on the river bank, his face contorted in agony. They are not my words; it was the description by the man who found him. An inquiry revealed that the bottle of poison which the man had placed in his fishing basket had spilled drops of its contents, apparently through a loosening of the tapered stopper, with the result that his sandwiches which were half eaten had been contaminated with a fatal dose of the cyanide.

The sequel to this story is that within a week of this tragedy steel fencing had been erected around the plant with warning notices plastered all round. But again no blame was attached to anyone - it was just an unfortunate accident.

The next serous health risk was the use of tricoethylene as a degreasing agent. It was kept in open tanks for use by workshop staff to clean components. Toxic fumes from this chemical, which the men inhaled as they leaned over the tanks, would cause dizzy spells and in some cases a collapse into unconsciousness. No one would think about the danger, it was only laughed about as a joke and the only precaution we were told to take was to take a step back and breathe deeply before you started to clean. Years later, the chemical was banned from all workshops and listed as a dangerous substance.

Steam pressure gauges which were repaired and calibrated in the shop were fitted with a brass rim. To remove the verdigris (a poisonous green oxidisation associated with copper and brass) from the rim they were dipped in a tank of sulphuric acid. They came out regaining their golden colour, but not without danger to the operator of the process or to the passers-by. A thick yellowish gas cloud would fill the surrounding air the instant the rims touched the acid. People in the vicinity would choke when inhaling the fumes. The labourer whose job it was to dip the rims while I worked in the department died a young man from the effects. Again no indication, signs or otherwise of the danger to health.

The events I am about to describe most people will think are rather childish. But when you are standing by a machine all day performing the same operations hour after hour, boredom sets in and you will do almost anything to relieve it. (Remember I was only about 18 at the time).

One pastime which produced plenty of laughs was to dip matchstick ends in grease, ensuring a good blob, and then flick it with the fingers at the machine operators opposite or at passers-by. The target was the cap but anywhere around the face caused great amusement.

As we all know, things like this tend to expand; weapons must increase in size. The maximum was attained the day I loaded a wooden arm splint with about half a pound of softish grease and aimed it spear-like at my old workmate and friend who was directly in line. It was a perfect hit; if I had gone and placed it on his head it could not have been more accurate. The grease started its path on the tip of the peak and traversed the curve of the hat at rapid speed to finish at the back of his neck. The man remained a workmate but not a friendly one.

Note that the majority of those who worked in the machining area were between 17 and 18 years of age so common sense did not always prevail. One day a rotten egg was placed in my machine's oil box. The awful smell permeated the surrounding area for days; passing workers gave queer looks at the machine's operator.

I searched every area around the machine but to no avail; it was not until I replenished the oil at the weekend that the source of the smell was discovered. This was a case of someone getting his own back. I suspected it was the grease-flirting incident but I could not complain. If you play a joke you must take one.

It was not always apprentices who played pranks. Sammy Mason, a little man nearing retirement, was always coming up with something unusual such as hanging pieces of bacon rind from his nose then approaching someone face to face. They would step back quickly in disgust. He would do the same with torch bulbs in his nostrils, but his favourite trick was to wrap pieces of soap in toffee papers and hand them out from a bag mostly to fresh starters in the department. The effects were very funny especially for those with false teeth, as the taste buds of those people did not react as rapidly as others with their own teeth.

Once, someone placed of a set of false teeth in a man's brew can where he had added tea previously. He filled the can with boiling water, added sugar and milk, poured the tea into a cup, together with the teeth. Not a happy man.

We would coat pennies with white metal to make them look like silver coins, solder a nail on one side and drive it into the wooden floor, then wait for someone passing to spot it. Many times someone would have a quick look round to see if anyone was watching, then take a dive down to snatch up the coin with the resulting loss of bits of finger nails. We even caught the shop foreman having a go, much to his embarrassment.

Some of us on nights would occasionally occupy a small unused office to have our meal break. One man had gone to cook himself bacon and eggs. While he was away someone placed a huge heavy ball of rope on top of the half open door.

Ron the cook returned holding a tin plate containing the meal in front of him, kicked open the door whereupon the rope dropped with force on the plate, tore it from Ron's hand and flattened the contents.

All hell was let loose. Ron, a six foot six giant, let out a roar of rage, jumped on all the various packets and bags of food and kicked and smashed all the cups. I was returning to the office with a mug of tea at the time and just missed the action. It was not me who placed the rope but it was me who had suggested that by doing so would cause a laugh. I can vouch that there was no merriment that night.

A final incident showing the unfeeling attitude of some was the night that a very nervous person was asleep full length in a box truck. Someone tied his legs together then shouted that the foreman was on his way. The poor man tried to leap to his feet, but restricted somewhat by the binding round his legs, fell flat on his face. He was surprised but otherwise unhurt.

Although the time spent in frivolity was necessary to keep peace of mind it was a very small part of the day, mainly just a few minutes. Most of the time was spent working really hard to accomplish the set number of components required to make the day's money. Each component was priced as little as one penny so a hundred Yorkshire couplings a day would just about pay the minimum bonus for the week.

The system of payment was called piecework. Every new item was timed by a man called a piecework setter. He would stand by your machine for probably half a day watching you work. If you worked too slowly he would tell you to speed up. The intention was to get as many items as possible in the shortest time. He would indicate at the end the amount that was necessary in a day. If you could exceed that amount, which was very unlikely, an increase in bonus was possible.

The bonus was an addition to the standard weekly rate that everyone on the job shared including the charge hand. Each workshop and department had differing amounts. The brass shop was the lowest in the whole Works.

This was a bone of contention for the brass shop workers and in fact it never changed over the following years. My take home pay at the age of 19 was less than three pounds a week which was about four or five shillings short of the Works' average.

One thing I could not abide with working on machines was standing for hours on one spot, so I never did. I would work furiously for about half an hour then wander, maybe to talk to other workmates or visit other departments. This would drive my charge hand wild when he saw that I was missing. He would walk up and down past my machine fuming, but we never had a real argument as he knew that at the end of the day I would complete my daily target.

My time in the brass shop was about to end. I was nearing the end of my apprenticeship with just one more move. The charge hand tried to retain me, but the period remaining before my 21st birthday was too great and permission was refused. I had enjoyed my stay there - if enjoyment is the right word. Let's say that it was better than any of the other shops I had worked in - and, of course, the experience was another notch on my bow.

Developments were then taking place within the Works, mainly the repair of diesel and electric locomotives and much later the start of new-build diesel electric high-speed locos. As the staff had little knowledge of these types, management decided to run a series of diesel courses. I attended these at the Works training school and also, in a quest for knowledge, I attended courses in 1965 at the local training college in my own time.

Before ending my first work experience in the brass shop I would like to describe some of the characters who worked there. Fred, a labourer, came by train from Stoke and found a packet of sandwiches on the train. He brought them into work and placed them in a cupboard. A week later I saw him open the packet and start eating the contents. When he saw I was watching, he strolled over to me and declared it was the best ham he had ever tasted!

He would bring water cress wrapped in newspaper and cress covered in yellow algae, stuff some in his cheese sandwiches and eat them with relish. Later when I teased him about his eating habits, he said he had served as a soldier with the Eighth Army in North Africa working in an army mortuary, laying out the soldier casualties. When you have been there he said, a bit of food poisoning means nothing.

Another chap, Harry, smoked 70 cigarettes a day one after the other - I usually smoked about 10. On one particular occasion, on night shift, I ran out of cigarettes just half an hour before finishing work at 8a.m. I asked him if he could lend me a fag until the next shift. Harry pulled his tin out of his pocket, opened it and said: 'I'm sorry, I've only got 10 left to last me until the shift ends.' Many years later I found Harry was still smoking when almost 90 years old.

If some of the practices and procedures within the Works were dubious, the welfare of the employees regarding sport was very good. A first class cricket ground was provided and many Test cricketers, both West Indian and English, played in charity matches on this ground. An inter-department cricket knock-out took place each year. This competition started me playing my favourite sport.

There was a sports club with an adjacent football pitch, with teams in local leagues. Badminton, tennis courts and bowling greens were also available. Darts, dominoes, billiards and snooker and many other interests were catered for. The LMR Dramatic Society produced two or three plays a year and my dear wife Kathleen, who also worked for the company, took part in many plays.

During the early years of the war and for a period after a concert was arranged at Christmas with workmates performing various acts. A stage was built in the Erecting Shop from metal plates. The one concert that sticks in my mind is a performance by Foden's Band, but the most amusing act was a member of the office staff performing year after year "I'll join the Legion" with the appropriate army dress uniform. This was taken from the musical "White Horse Inn". It was the comedy act of the show when he sang "I'll do or die, you'll know the reason why" – the crowd erupted. The third verse goes:

*In some Abyssinian French Dominion*
*I shall do my bit,*
*And fall for the flag if I must.*
*Where the desert sand is nice and handy,*
*I'll be full of grit;*
*You won't see my heels for the dust.*
*I'll do or die*
*You'll know the reason why*
*When told of bold Leopold's "last stand"*
*For the Fatherland*

# CHAPTER 9

## Finally qualified as a fitter

The dreaded day of the next and final move eventually arrived - bearing in mind that wherever my last placing was to be, I could end up at the age of 21 with a permanent position there.

I was told to report to the Erecting Shop office where I was directed to the last stage of repair on belt five. The first person I met there was my future brother-in-law, Jabez Blackburn.

The work involved was the final completion of repair of the steam loco before being despatched for the testing of the vacuum brake system and controls. My particular job was the fitting of the axle box 'keeps' which secured the wheels in position. This was a heavy task as each keep weighed about 90lbs and required two men to position. What made the job more difficult was that we would be bent double in the pit under the loco - as you can imagine, backache was an occupational hazard.

After a few months I was put to work on the final coupling of the valve gear motion. This connected all the necessary bits and pieces to do with the supply of the steam to the pistons and control over the forward and reverse function. (This is a simplified explanation of a quite complicated system.)

About this time I was nearing my 21st birthday, the last few days of my apprenticeship. The decision was about to be made about my position when becoming a fully-fledged tradesman. When you finished your apprenticeship and if your charge hand liked your work record, both in quality and quantity, he tried to keep you on his job, but only providing it did not exceed his staff quota.

As the big day approached, I was told to report to the Works Manager's office where I was interviewed by Mr. O'Neil, the under manager, who supervised apprentice training. He talked about my record during the last seven years, with just one little blot, the suspension. He congratulated me on the good reports from all my workplaces, but asked for an explanation about my suspension. I told him the facts, saying that I thought it was a harsh decision because I had finished my work quota for the day and as no one was available to issue me with a permit to leave my shop I proceeded to my previous department not thinking of the consequences. I further told him about the method of my receiving the suspension notice (including the foreman's trip from the theatre) and that at least made him laugh.

Then, to my surprise, he said he would delete the suspension from my records, not because I was innocent but due to the ridiculous way that I was notified. He issued me with a certificate confirming my trade qualifications which were in engineering fitting and turning and he also said that I would be remaining in my present position as a fitter.

So that was the decision. It was not ideal; it could have meant me working on the same job possibly for my whole working life or at least in the same department. However, I decided to settle down to the task but with the thought of applying for any other moves that were suitable. My aim was to return to the brass shop where I would be reasonably happy; also because of my experience there I thought I would have a chance to gain promotion to a staff position.

One ritual which occurred when an apprentice finished his seven year training was the Chamber Pot Event. The pot had a big eye painted inside and was suspended upside down high up in the roof girders. The newly qualified tradesman had to climb up a ladder which was sometimes greased to make the exercise more difficult. The pot was wired to the girders making the time taken to release it quite lengthy. When the pot was returned to the shop floor the unfortunate young man was thoroughly smeared with grease over his face and overalls

My first duty as a fully-fledged fitter was again assembling the heavy metal steel 'keeps' which secured the wheels to the loco frame, but this time I was in charge of an apprentice myself and responsible for the quality of the work. It was a good thought, too, knowing that at the end of the day I didn't have to clean the tools.

Over the next two or three years I was engaged in all the various tasks to do with the final repair functions of a steam locomotive - fitting driver controls which included the regulator lever, vacuum brake valves, water injectors, water level sight glasses, steam pressure gauges and vacuum gauges. Also the many other bits and pieces to complete the function of the valves supplying steam to the pistons.

An incident I must mention, some might find a little amusing, although it was certainly not to the recipient. Part of the valve mechanism was a large casting called an expansion link. It had to be fitted in a precise manner and lifted by the fitter to matching holes in the loco frame. His apprentice would scan the holes and when these were correctly lined up he would fit a pin to secure the link. But on this day the lad poked his finger in the hole to ensure a good match and said the positioning was OK, whereupon the fitter who thought the pin had been placed in position dropped the link and sliced off the boy's finger.

As I have mentioned previously I was at times working on this job with my future brother-in-law, Jabe Blackburn. During normal conversation we discussed where we spent our leisure time. Jabe said that on a Sunday night he and his girlfriend went to the Irish dances, held in the local dance hall in the Corn Exchange. He told me that his girlfriend Barbara had a sister named Kathleen and if I would like to meet her he could arrange a date. I agreed that I would go to the dance the following Sunday where we could meet as a foursome.

My first sight of Kathleen was to say at the least very impressionable. She was a lovely-looking brown haired girl with a bubbly personality - just my type. We got on famously from this first meeting and later arranged to see each other again. From then on the romance blossomed and after a lovely courtship we were married about 18 months later. (I have got carried away a little here).

At the age of 23 I was desperate to be transferred to another department. I had stated my preference for the brass shop because it did not include the hard manual work that my present job entailed and   This was the real reason for a move.

My Father had bought a farm in Broughton Road, Crewe, and required my assistance to run it but which I would be unable to do if I arrived home every day dog tired. My commitment to dad was very important to me. He had secured the farm for me when he retired, so although it did not work out like that for many reasons it was with the best of intentions.

Now I started my efforts to gain a transfer. I contacted my old workmates in the brass shop to see how the land lay. They informed me that personnel had changed, the old charge hand had retired and a new one had been appointed named Bob Hough who was quite a good friend of mine. (I later found that his real name was Cyril)

I then found out that there was to be a vacancy in the coming months and if I applied I could possibly get the job. Bob did get in touch with me and said he wanted me to work for him and that he had put my name forward, so it was wait and see. Many will wonder why I was so insistent on gaining a position in that department, but apart from the light work it was the premier place to work in and most men would have been over the moon to get a job in there.

Months passed with no news until the day I had a visit from, by now, my best friend, charge hand, Bob. He informed me that I was to be transferred to his job in the brass shop the following Monday. So, at the age of 23, I had achieved my objective.

Outside the Erecting Shop with cross traverser in foreground c1970

HST Power Car 43158

Wheels for electric locos c1970s

Welding Wagon Frames

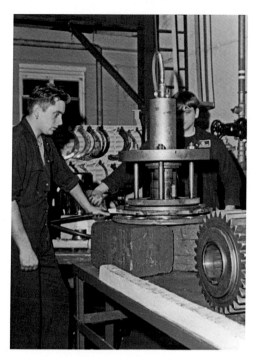

Gearing for Electric Locos

Axle assembly for electric loco

Grinding valves for diesel loco

Diesel Engine being conveyed by
crane to the Locomotive

Class 08 Diesel shunter arrives by low loader for repairs

Bogie repairs for electric loco

Welding electric loco chassis

Electric loco roof construction

Wheel balancing for electric loco

Diesel engine on freight wagon

Francis Trevithick's 2-2-2 No.3020 "Cornwall" was one of the earliest engines built at Crewe in 1847. It was rebuilt by Ramsbottom in 1858 and was in regular LNWR service until 1902. It was then utilised to haul the CME's Inspection saloon until 1925. Now preserved for static display by the National Railway Museum at York. Note the large 8 feet 6 inch driving wheels

Stanier "Black Five" 4-6-0 5305 (now preserved) seen outside the works for hot axlebox repairs.

Inside cab of 5305

Cowans Sheldon 75t Breakdown Crane. These were located at some of the largest motive power depots and used at mishaps and derailments or places where heavy lifting was required.

New Class 91 Electra Loco on lift

BR Electric No.91031 "Sir Henry Royce" was the last locomotive to be built in Crewe Works. Seen outside the Works with staff in February 1991

91031 "Sir Henry Royce" was the last of the Electra Class which was a very powerful loco of 6,480hp with a maximum speed of 140mph (225km/h). They were designed for the IC225 trains on the East Coast route.

Queen's Park, Crewe in 2018 showing the main entrance lodge and clock tower. The park was a gift to the town by the LNWR in 1887

Autumn in Queen's Park, Crewe - one of the most attractive in the North West

"Gaffers Row" in Delamere Street, Crewe 2018,
LNWR Houses built for the Work's Foremen

Workmen's houses built by LNWR c1848 in Tollitt Street, Crewe.
They would have been luxurious for families moving from Liverpool.
Now fully restored for private use.

71000 4-6-2 "Duke of Gloucester" built in 1952, designed by Robert Riddles
seen at Crewe Works Open Day 2005

4 restored Stanier Pacifics 46233 "Duchess of Sutherland, 46229 "Duchess of
Hamilton", 46203 "Princess Margaret Rose" and 46201 "Princess Elizabeth"
at Crewe Works Open Day 2005

46203 "Princess Margaret Rose" built 1935 at Crewe Works Open Day 2005

46441 LMS Ivatt 2-6-0 built 1949 and 48151 Stanier 8F 2-8-0 built 1942
at Crewe Works Open Day 2005

87035 BR 5,000hp Electric Locomotive "Robert Burns"
built 1974, on hoist at Crewe Works Open Day 2005

Stanier 6229 "Duchess of Hamilton" now restored with original streamlined
casing seen at York National Railway Museum 2017

6229 "Duchess of Hamilton" nameplate at York 2017

Inside the cab of 6229 "Duchess of Hamilton"

Crewe Works "Cab" seen in earlier photo of the 1913 royal visit now fully restored at Crewe Heritage Centre 2018

# CHAPTER 10

## Back to brass, politics and trade unions

I was now in the department where I was to spend the longest period of my working career. I had returned to machining, the difference this time was that I had to set up my own lathe to the drawing requirements. When I was an apprentice an appointed trade turner setter would have to do it for me.

Over a long period, I operated most of the department's machines: centre lathes, turret lathes and capstan lathes, mainly producing complicated brass casting components used in the injector and ejector, the main valves supplying water to the loco boiler. Most of the time I worked 'fortnights about', days and nights. The nights were long and boring but brought about some very amusing incidents. There was no foreman based in the department on nights but a patrolling foreman would visit on a regular basis (he was also responsible for four other shops.) The visits were always at the same time which allowed us to relax for periods away from the machines.

Then came a change of personnel - an older incompetent foreman who thought that a change would somehow increase production. He firstly introduced himself: 'Call me Mr Dobson', he said. He then informed us that he would come and visit at any time and he expected to find us all working at our machines, apart from the breaks. This comment did not go down well and the staff decided to get a little bit of our own back on him the next night.

The entrance to the shop was through a small door set inside a much larger one. Fishing line was tied across the top of the small door and just inside the entrance another piece was secured between two pillars. At the top of a flight of stairs which led to the shop office a line was also placed across the door jambs.

With the men waiting in anticipation, Mr Dobson, wearing the traditional foreman's bowler hat had it whipped from his head as he passed through the small entrance door. Giving a sickly grin as he replaced it and passing between the pillars he again was deprived of his headgear. This obviously upset him; he marched swiftly feeling his way as he climbed to the top of the stairs. He stopped and faced down to the shop, shook his fist, turned and passed through the door. The bowler came off and bounced down the stairs. We expected repercussions but after interviewing about 40 of us he gave up the ghost. But from that night he reverted back to the old visit times.

Some of the men on nights would bring various pies to eat in the dinner break. They were eaten cold as there were no means provided to warm them except on this particular night. One person had what he thought was a brilliant idea. Large urns were used to provide boiling water for the brews. The tops of these were about 18 inches across, fitted with a lid. So someone put their big meat and potato pie in a paper bag and put it on this convenient heat source. Joe, a labourer who was the water 'topper-upper' of the urns from a tap above, lifted the lid without moving the paper bag. The unfortunate outcome of this was that the tea and coffee subsequently made from the urn also held a mixture of meat, carrots, potatoes and the soggy remains of a brown paper bag. No wonder the pie owner got a drenching as most of the undrinkable mess was thrown over him.

Quite a scandal occurred in the department concerning distribution of food parcels from Australia during the war period. The Australian people provided these for needy workers, mainly with large families. The shop organising committee, who were responsible for this, decided that they were the needy and kept them for themselves. Resignations were rife; the committee members were disbanded with dishonour.

During the war about 100 women worked in the department operating apprentice machinery, turning small components such as tail pipes and small brass nuts and bolts. But the majority worked on the benches mostly removing burrs and assembling parts.

The lady who represented the women was my cousin, Edith Stubbs, whose brother obviously another cousin, also worked nearby on a machine. I have mentioned before about women being conscientious workers especially on machines but with just one failing. Some could not gauge the speed and pressure that was required to drill into metal. Scores of drills were broken which drove the setters to distraction. I suppose without training of working with metal, the task was sometimes difficult for them.

A move from the boredom of operating machines was my next job of interest - the maintenance and repair of plant and machinery. Some of the intricate gearbox systems were hard to fathom but with the aid of machine drawings it was possible to locate faults. The man who called on me to do this work was the charge hand responsible for all maintenance - he was a bit eccentric and not very clever. He would ask me to get involved when an urgent repair was required and the knowledge I obtained from this work would lead to my future promotion.

Many of the machines at this time were automatics which meant that they were set up to turn, drill, screw and part off components without the constant attention of an operator. The only function he performed while looking after three machines was to feed them with metal bars.

The constant leg pulling between man and apprentice was evident in many ways. For instance, asking the boy to go to the tool stores for a left handed spanner, or a double handed screwdriver. But one boy retaliated by heating the fitter's spanner on the gas stove while he was at the toilet - the result can be imagined.

Another time when the tables were turned was when a fitter who was gasping for a fag asked a boy to go to the local shop in the dinner break for a packet of Players cigarettes. As the boy took his money he said: 'What if they don't have any Players?' The man told him to 'bring anything.' So the lad returned with four packets of crisps and two bottles of lemonade!

In 1952 I was 24 and the most important event in my life was my marriage to Kathleen on the 29th March. Kathleen was 19 and there were those who said jokingly it was case of kidnapping. But we were both very happy, had a lovely wedding, honeymooned in London and settled down to our life at Holly Tree Farm.

Kathleen and her dad were both employed by the Railway Company. Kath worked in the general offices as a clerical officer and Albert, her dad was a blacksmith in the outstation department.

One of the most enjoyable things about my long period in this shop were the political arguments. It appeared to me that 99.9% of the staff were Labour voters. I loved the repartee with the three Labour town councillors and shop steward who worked nearby. I had joined the Conservative Trade Union Movement and received a monthly newsletter. The first edition I plastered alongside the union pamphlets on the shop notice board.

The shop steward approached me and demanded that I remove my notices. I replied that I would do so if he removed his. During a brief discussion the foreman arrived on the scene. I stated my case; both were union literature so both should remain. The foreman agreed, but as I walked past the board later my newsletter had been removed - so much for democracy.

Now just a funny tale about a young fitter who would come to work each morning with a box full of fancy cream cakes. These were handed out to all the men on his job. They didn't say anything for quite a while, thinking that as long as they were not stolen, it would be best to leave alone.

But, eventually, curiosity overcame good sense and he was asked outright where he got them from. 'Well', he said, 'at the back of my house in Congleton there is a baking company and alongside it is a rubbish dump. The cakes I bring in are not stolen, they are piled on this dump and anyone can help themselves.' There were a few men heaving at the thought, especially when they were informed that the dump was riddled with rats.

# CHAPTER 11

## A new diesel era begins - and promotion beckons

At this point in my career I was offered a new position in the brake valve repair section. This was important and demanding work, especially with the advent of diesel and electric locomotives in addition to the steam locos. The new repair function was a break from the old practices - modern methods were becoming the order of the day.

Every engineering tradesman had to attend a fortnight's 'Diesel Appreciation Course' at the training school where there was a sample of diesel engines of various types available. Rolls Royce, English Electric and Rushton Paxton diesels were the main types. Tuition was given on the principal and operation of the diesel engine, together with maintenance details.

I also had a fortnight at the British Rail Training College at Derby on the repair of diesel and electric locomotive braking systems and a four weeks diesel course at Derby School of Transport. To complete the training process I attended two other courses; a four-week course on mechanical and electrical supervision at Derby and a two-year evening diesel course at Crewe College of Further Education.

It was an eye opener, especially for the older men brought up to repair steam locos. The old fitting process whereby parts were actually made to fit by the skill of the fitter no longer applied. Diesel components were supplied by the engine manufactures to very fine tolerance; no added work was required apart from assembly.

Personally, I was very keen to absorb all I was told and the scope for advancement to a more satisfying position became evident. Apart from the engines, there were the huge electric generators producing power to the loco bogie traction motors and the alternators for all other auxiliary electrical supplies. There were complicated brake systems, both vacuum and rheostat and air operated sophisticated warning equipment that stopped the loco automatically when danger was indicated. These and thousands of other components were entirely new to Crewe Works staff.

When people refer to engines they mostly talk in respect of car engines, but the sheer size of a main-line 3,500hp locomotive diesel engine is awesome. The 8, 12 or 16 pistons are approximately 12 inches in diameter. The crankshafts are 10 feet in length and weigh about four tons. When ticking over in neutral mode the engine vibrates the whole 100-ton locomotive.

The above descriptions are only the bare bones of the complicated structure of a diesel loco, but just enough to indicate the complexity of this new type of work practice that would be required.

Beginning my new work on brake valves the number of the various types was well over a hundred. They were mostly manufactured by Westinghouse and Davies & Metcalfe and required different methods of test and repair.

When I started, only a small amount of valves were to hand due to the trickle of diesel and electric locos coming in initially for repair. Very little was known about the repair and testing of the valves and although the manufacturers manuals were available these were couched in technical terms. So although attempts were made to repair successfully most valves failed the test.

The charge hand on the job took me into the test plant and showed me a great pile of valves that had failed the test requirements through the lack of knowledge by the fitting staff. He said: 'If you think you can correct this failure situation start with this lot'. To say that I solved the problems at the drop of a hat would be wrong. First, I took home the repair and test manuals and spent hours going through in detail all the necessary fine adjustments to ensure a fair chance of a successful test. Then I had a number of small test rigs made to enable me to try the numerous working parts within the valves individually, before the complete item was tested.

Over the next weeks, after a few hiccups, tests on 95% of the major brake valves were successful. I was really pleased with the outcome, as were the people that had struggled to overcome the problems previously, including so called experts of the Technical and Inspection staff.

Now I was consulted to explain to the rest of the staff the necessary attention to detail that was required. This was because, although they were capable of performing the tasks eventually, the learning curve from the old fitting practices died hard. The fact that I was in at the start of this new type of work was a big advantage and would lead me into a real chance of promotion.

The Finished Work Inspector who was responsible for overseeing and signing for the completed correct test results approached me. After quizzing me about a few of the improvements that I had instigated he asked if I would be interested in a temporary inspection position.

This was to be my introduction to a supervisory post. It would mean that I, together with the appointed Staff Inspector would examine all the work repaired in the department and sign to verify conformity to drawings and specifications. Brake systems were not the only components repaired here. There were heat exchangers, hydraulic pipe work, water injectors and ejectors, pantographs, circuit breakers, vacuum gauges, pressure gauges as well as all the numerous brass items fitted to a loco.

All the above items required specific repair requirements to the relative procedures. All were subjected to rigorous tests which were monitored and verified by the inspection staff.

# CHAPTER 12

## How I saved the company a fortune

The 70 or so machines in the brass shop manufactured all the new brass bushes required for the locomotives as well as refurbishing repairable items. Naturally, all of these items had to be inspected for flaws and sized to the relevant specification or drawing. Inspection and testing of the circuit breakers was a lengthy process involving critical timings for the opening and closing of the contacts. These large electrical switches were fitted on the roof of electric locos where a pantograph was used to transfer power from the overhead lines via the circuit breaker to the traction motors.

During inspection of parts while the breakers were being repaired I noticed that one particular item was being renewed every time - a very expensive pure copper fixed contact, (not the tiny contacts you would find in a household switch but these were 120cm long, 45cm diameter, with a 20cm bore, of silver coated copper.)

The moving contact was fired into the fixed contact by compressed air thereby making the circuit, but this operation would eventually create a deep crater that caused the piece of equipment to be scrapped.

I submitted a repair method through the company staff suggestions scheme. I reckoned a copper insert could be fitted quite simply into the contact, which I was able to oversee because part of my duties were the inspection and test of this component. Further still, I also simulated thousands of operations on the test bed to prove that my method of refurbishment would comply with the technical data. This repair method would save the company thousands of pounds annually.

Two years after the submission I had heard nothing from the staff suggestions committee apart from a letter acknowledging receipt of my repair method. Shortly after this period the Chief Electrical Engineer of British Rail visited the department to look at some new equipment and I approached him with my idea, plus a sample drawing and test results. He studied them for a few moments, turned to his assistant and instructed him to pursue the matter immediately.

He apologised for the delay, saying that he would personally oversee its progress. Lo and behold, a month later I was awarded £3,500 for the best suggestion of the year and a chance to travel to the British Rail Headquarters in London to be presented with the cheque by the British Rail Chairman, Sir Peter Parker. Unfortunately I was ill and off work on the precise day so I missed out. A few days later, however, I got a letter from him saying that he hoped I would soon recover and that he was sorry to have missed meeting me.

Another suggestion I submitted was for a reduction of parts in the main line diesel loco drivers' brake valves. All of the valves were duplicated in European locomotives which involved very high air pressures because of steep inclines and descents. The British Rail tracks were level so the high pressure section in the valves was not required. My idea eventually removed up to 40 components from a single valve with a combined saving per year of £100,000.

For this suggestion I received £50 and a BR pen. It seemed to me that because BR technical staff had not seen this discrepancy, it was kept very quiet and low key.

A short time after this suggestion was submitted a representative from the manufacturers of the valves, Westinghouse Brake Company, who I had met many times, came to see me and said: 'Why didn't you tell me when you discovered the parts were not needed, we could then have come to some agreement. The reduction of parts will cost our company thousands of pounds.'

Around this period, after I had completed a couple of years as a temporary inspector, the department's permanent finished work inspector retired. The position was advertised throughout the Works so it meant that every temporary inspector in the fitting trade could apply for this job and about 100 were eligible. An application form was supplied to each man, where qualifications, work history, good time keeping and knowledge of the specific work were to be indicated.

Although I was quietly confident of achieving this position there was a problem. The foreman of the department and I had had many disagreements due mainly to the fact that he wanted me to sign for work, including the payment which I was responsible for, that had not actually been completed. This I would not do, not wanting to jeopardise my position with the possibility of dismissal if the powers that be found out.

So that was the scenario. When I was on holiday this foreman nominated one of his favourites to the position in an effort to undermine me, keeping him on after I returned to work. The situation got so serious that I decided to ask for an interview with the chief inspector to clarify the situation.

What the foreman did not know was that the chief was an old school mate of mine, Wilf Madely. After a couple of minutes talk with Wilf in his office, we marched back to the department where the foreman was given a dressing down and told in no uncertain terms by someone in upper management not to interfere with his staff, temporary or not.

From that time through to my interview a month later there were no problems. So in 1971 I was interviewed by a panel of four managers (including the under manager) and mainly due to my qualifications and experience was appointed as a member of the Permanent Inspection Staff. I have got to admit though that Wilf, one of the panellists, gave me a wink as I walked into the interview room. This was the first permanent step on the promotion ladder with all the added perks, such as shorter working hours, a superannuated pension scheme and more authority which suited me down to the ground.

With meeting and talking to other department supervisors and shop foremen, I was asked on many occasions to act as temporary foreman in their departments when others were off, due to leave and illness. Although the components were manufactured differently, the duties such as discipline and production requirements were similar.

Over the next few years, apart from the normal repair and production requirements of steam locomotives things changed dramatically. The repair of diesel locomotives had started and later the building of the High Speed Train, capable of 125mph. British Rail, which was previously the London Midland & Scottish Railway Company, became British Rail Engineering Ltd, independent of the government. This meant it could negotiate for other contracts, apart from locomotive repair and build programs with private companies.

One of the many changes was the supreme importance of quality to comply with British standards. A few years previously the old imperial standard was changed to metric. This caused confusion, whereby we had measurements like 'sixty three sixty fourths'. The metric system was relatively simple, but tell that to the older fitting staff. They had to be given tuition on the changes and metric measuring equipment was issued, but confusion and opposition were retained over a number of years. Change can sometimes be a slow business.

Changes in quality requirements were undertaken by an independent company. They placed the responsibility for quality on the working staff, in other words 'built in quality', as opposed to inspecting for quality after the work had been done. This meant that many inspectors were surplus to requirements. I was lucky, my boss had earmarked me for a position in the standards room where all measuring equipment was calibrated, a super clean air-conditioned environment.

To me this move was just what I wanted, working with sophisticated modern calibration equipment to set the required tolerances for all the various test and inspection items used in the workshops. Again it also gave me a chance to gain promotion by meeting people in authority.

The head of the main machine shop asked me if I was interested in a temporary foreman's position. I said I was and I did periods in that department as foreman. I also did six months as the superintendent on nights responsible for production and discipline. It was quite a daunting task controlling 1,500 men.

You can never bank on human nature, either. This was brought home to me when a workman came to me on nights telling tales that a certain person was sleeping under the bed of his machine. This could lead to a three day suspension for sleeping on duty. In some instances the men were the mates who worked alongside them. I rooted the sleeper out with a warning. In the old days it would have been unthinkable for this to happen as no one reported anyone. But now I thought of the time when I, too, used to work on the shop floor.

An incident which made me smile afterwards occurred when I was supervising in the foundry. Kathleen and I were on Stalybridge Station waiting to catch a train to York when onto the platform came three men who worked for me. The look on their faces when they saw me was something to behold - a clear look of guilt.

Obviously they were taking the day off which was not a holiday, hoping to put a sick note in on the following day. I remarked that I did not remember signing their leave forms. Anyway I told them

130

(being the kindly person I am) that I wanted to see three leave chits from them in the morning. They could have been disciplined, of course, but they were excellent workers and even better after that episode.

# CHAPTER 13

## Appointed works quality auditor

Although I was happy in the standards room, it was not the long term position that I wanted. My boss, the chief inspector, informed me that a new position, quality auditor, was being advertised. The duties were mainly ensuring that all calibration parameters were met both within the works and also with outside suppliers and that quality procedures and testing were to the British Standard specification 5750. At that time I applied for the position along with dozens of other hopeful candidates - and I was successful. It meant I received uplift in grade equivalent to a department chief foreman.

I was based in the main Headquarters BREL House, in the quality manager's office. About a week later I was at Derby attending another training course. This was a hard and intensive two weeks; the auditor manual was full of auditor procedures and methods of investigating quality failures. Even at the end of the day in my hotel room I would be going through the details into the late hours. The last day of the course was a written exam with a qualifying pass rate of 85%. Thankfully, the result was given to me a week later with a pass.

My first duties in this new position were to visit every manufacturing department looking at component quality procedures to ensure that the required parameters had been met. Workshop staff had to be questioned regarding the use and understanding of the procedures. All measuring equipment was examined to make sure that they had been calibrated within the period allowed.

Written reports of the results from each department were directed to the Quality Manager. The satisfaction that came with carrying out this job was knowing that all involved in the manufacturing process - staff, shop foreman and even managers were obliged to correct any discrepancies that I had found without argument.

Not only did I audit within Crewe works, but I also audited at Derby Loco Works and visited many outside firms and companies manufacturing components for our use to ensure that items we received were to the required British Standard specification 5750.

One very interesting change from my normal daily duties was a talk I gave in Derby on automatic and rheostat braking systems to a party of chief railway engineers from South Africa, India and some of the far Eastern States. This was arranged through an organisation called 'Transmark' who ran educational talks for under-developed countries.

I was quite nervous when I realised who the audience was - the big bosses of the Indian, Egyptian and South African railways to name a few. But once I had introduced myself there was no problem mainly because of my experience of working on and studying brake systems over a number of years.

I smile to myself when I recall this incident during my talk. After about an hour the Egyptian manager remarked in a sarcastic voice that he knew all about the brake systems I was describing. I replied: 'If you think you know it all there's no point in your staying - you know where the door is.' Quite a number of the other engineers reiterated what I had said and told him to leave but, looking quite embarrassed, he remained in his chair. When at the end of the talk I was issuing them all with a host of printed details, I purposefully ignored him and passed by. He said: 'Mr Skellon you have missed me!' I replied; 'Yes, I did. You seem to know it all!'

I was congratulated afterwards by the whole class for a very instructive talk and also by the Transmark observer who was very impressed with the way I had dealt with the arrogant Egyptian - the best part of my day!

# CHAPTER 14

## An instructor in the workshops

Due to problems with locomotive brake equipment repair and testing, I was asked to prepare an instruction manual with precise details for the use of personnel engaged in that process. After completion this I ran a weekly instruction course in the training school with classes of 20 people over a period of 6 months. Mostly I enjoyed teaching. Some of the best times were when lots of questions were asked about specific problems, then with demonstrations to indicate the cure, took quite a time. At times like these it was difficult to finish the curriculum within the five days, but at other times when pupils were not quite so inquisitive it was a bit of a struggle to make the course last four days.

I spent many hours instructing in the workshops later. Due to the repair problems with brake systems, some of the older men who had been transferred from other repair departments where the work involved more heavy engineering, did not have the skill or aptitude required to repair sensitive equipment.

Each department had different requirements in regard to work procedures, test and calibration of measuring equipment. I would look at work procedures and repaired items to confirm that conditions were being met. I examined all test and measuring equipment for the correct calibration status and observed that the repaired components were stored and protected while awaiting despatch to other departments.

Each department or workshop was given a date when an audit was forthcoming. I knew that panic stations were in evidence in most departments with people desperately trying to get things in order before my arrival. Managers and foremen would phone me asking for delays, but to no avail.

# CHAPTER 15

## Two jobs for the price of one and retirement

There now came a time in my employment when changes were made due to a reduction in the company's workload, with the result that many positions were lost, a lot of people were given redundancy payments to retire early. As a consequence, those of us remaining took on additional work.

The quality engineer on my section was given an appointment as a chief foreman. I was asked to fill his position for a few weeks meaning that I would be covering two jobs; quality engineer and quality auditor. My responsibilities were the overseeing of the finished work inspection staff both at the Crewe and Derby railway workshops.

Sometime later, I was asked by the works manager if I would be interested in overseeing the repair of track maintenance vehicles. He said I had been recommended by one of his department managers. A separate workshop would be built within the Works to accommodate the repair and I would be in direct control. I looked at the prospectus and the job implications, which included extensive travel to the German firm who manufactured the new vehicles, plus visits to railway depots to see them operating. I decided that the time was not right for me when it was on my mind about taking voluntary redundancy.

I was offered other positions over the last few years of my employment with the chance of another managerial grade but the day came when I decided to apply for voluntary redundancy. It was turned down immediately by my boss the quality manager. He said he could not let me go at this time as he was being pressurised by management and wanted me to support him.

I applied again a few months later and this time he could not stop me, but he asked me as a favour, when I was granted my redundancy, would I continue in my job as a consultant for a short period. This I agreed to do and I worked for another six weeks.

And so, in 1992 and at the age of 63, I finally retired after 50 years with the company. This meant I had time to spend with my lovely wife Kathleen and daughters Jill and Gay, to go on holiday when and where I wanted with my family and friends.

I have written this account of my employment on the railway in 2010, 18 years after retirement. The memories are still vivid to this day and will always remain with me.

(Finally updated 2018)

# APPENDIX

On the following pages are details of Crewe Works history also Plans of Crewe's Old Works and Steel Works.

# CREWE LOCOMOTIVE WORKS
## Historical Notes

1843    The building of Crewe Works was commenced to serve as the Locomotive Works of the Grand Junction Railway Company and to take the place of the Liverpool Edge Hill Shops. The work was carried out under the supervision of Francis Trevithick who was appointed the first Locomotive Superintendent. At that time the area covered 2½ acres and the staff employed numbered 161 men.

1845    First Locomotive, 2-2-2 No.49 "Columbine", completed. Now preserved in the National Railway Museum in York.

1846    Taken over as the Works of the London & North Western Railway Company (LNWR)

1862    The Wolverton Works of the old London & Birmingham Railway was closed so far as locomotives were concerned and the construction and maintenance of all locomotives for the London & North Western Railway Company was transferred to Crewe Works under the control of John Ramsbottom who was appointed Locomotive Superintendent. The Works ultimately occupied an area of some 30 acres, known as the "Old Works".

1864    Bessemer Steel Plant opened

1866    1000th locomotive completed DX class 0-6-0 No.613

1865-
1880    During this period, the development of the "Steel Works" and the "Deviation Works" took place. The initial development at the Steel Works was the provision of a Bessemer Steel Plant which was later replaced by open hearth furnaces, the final plant consisting of two 45-ton and two 70-ton furnaces. Associated with the steel plant were the forge and rolling mills which produced standard sections and 60 foot permanent way rails until closed down in 1932. The whole of this plant has now been displaced.

With the increase in the size of locomotives it became necessary to provide larger workshops and steps were taken to meet this requirement. The Deviation Works was built after the Chester line had been deviated from its original route through the Works to one outside the boundary. This section of the Works provided accommodation for a Joiner's Shop, Saw Mill and Iron Foundry, the latter subsequently becoming the Millwright's Shop. Incidentally, the foregoing explains the adoption of the name "Deviation" which puzzles many visitors to the Works.

1876 Opening of the General Offices which provided accommodation for the Works Manager and his staff and also housed associated departments. The building, which was slightly curved, was almost central with the Works and 525 feet long.

1876 2000th locomotive completed - Webb 2-4-0T No.233

1887 3000th locomotive completed – 2-2-2-2T Webb compound No. 600

1888 0-6-0 No.2153 assembled in 25½ hours – a world record

1881- In the years prior to 1923 (in which year the London & North
1923 Western Railway became a constituent of the London Midland & Scottish Railway) extensions of various sections of the Steel Works were undertaken and, during this period, the whole of the Fitting and Erecting Shop work was transferred from the Old Works to the Steel Works.

1900 4000th locomotive completed - Jubilee class 4-4-0 No.1926 "La France"

1911 5000th locomotive completed - George the Fifth class 4-4-0 No.5000 "Coronation"

1925 A major reorganisation scheme was carried out involving the provision of a new Erecting Shop capable of dealing with the largest locomotives. Other features of this scheme were the adaption of the Old Works Erecting Shops as the new boiler building department and the rearrangement of the various sections resulting in self-contained Shops available for frame and cylinder work, tube repairs, brass finishing, welding and cutting, and stores.

1930 6000th locomotive built – Hughes 2-6-0 No.13178

1933 The first locomotive of the "Princess Royal" 4-6-2 class designed by Sir William Stanier, built at Crewe.

| 1930s | Numerous other Stanier Locos built including the highly successful Black Five 4-6-0s, Jubilees and Royal Scot classes also the 8F 2-8-0 freight engines |
|---|---|
| 1940s | During World War 2 many women were employed and the works built 161 Covenanter tanks for the Army. |
| 1950 | 7000th locomotive built – Ivatt class 2, 2-6-2T No. 41272 |
| 1951 | The first of the BR Standard Locomotives, a class 7, 4-6-2 No.70000 "Britannia" designed by R.A. Riddles was built. |
| 1951-1958 | Many BR Standard class steam locomotives built at Crewe culminating in their last - a class 9F 2-10-0 No.92250 on 31st December 1958 |
| 1957 | First diesel locomotive built 0-6-0 shunter No.D3419 |
| 1959 | First main line diesel electric class 24 No.D5030 built followed by many more including over 200 class 47s. |
| 1962 | Crewe works becomes part of BR Workshops Division |
| 1967 | Last class 47 diesel electric loco completed No.D1111 |
| 1967 | Last steam locomotive to be repaired – Britannia class 4-6-2 No.70013 "Oliver Cromwell" |
| 1969 | Crewe Works becomes part of British Rail Engineering Ltd (BREL) |
| 1973 | First class 87 electric locomotive built No.87001 followed by 35 more |
| 1975-1982 | Power Cars constructed for the famous HST (High Speed Trains) total 197 for the InterCity services nationwide. |
| 1978 | 8000th locomotive completed - HST power car No.43081 |
| 1987 | Class 90 electric locomotive construction commenced |
| 1988 | First class 91 electric locomotive built (as sub-contract for GEC) |
| 1989 | BREL privatised and sold to Swedish-Swiss Company ASEA Brown-Boveri (ABB). |
| 1991 | Last loco built in February No.91031 'Sir Henry Royce' |
| 1996 | ABB merged with Daimler-Benz to form Adtranz. |
| 2001 | Adtranz taken over by Canadian company Bombardier |

**BUILDINGS** By 2018 the Old Works and many other buildings had been demolished and replaced by roads, 2 supermarkets and houses.
**STAFF**
At its peak Crewe Works employed over 20,000 men and women but in 2018 this was down to only 350.

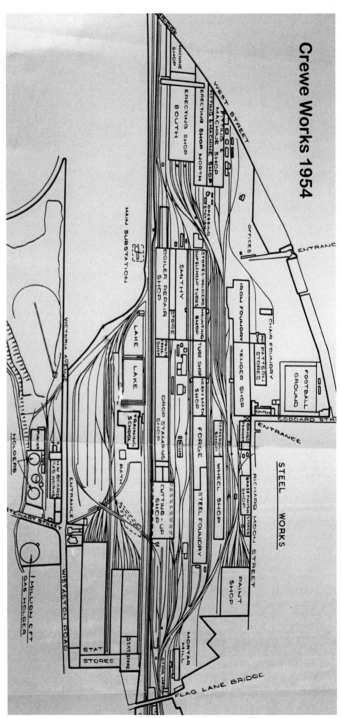

Crewe Works 1954

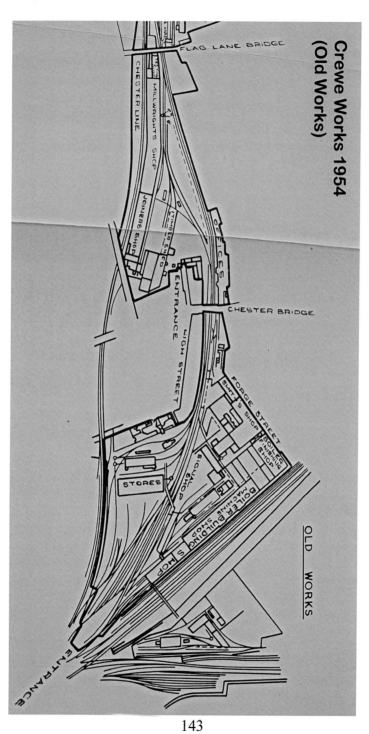

Crewe Works 1954 (Old Works)

FLAG LANE BRIDGE
CHESTER LINE
MILLWRIGHTS SHOP
JOINERS SHOP
TIMBER SHED
OFFICES
ENTRANCE
CHESTER BRIDGE
HIGH STREET
FORGE STREET
SMITHS SHOP
BOILER FINISHING SHOP
SIGNAL SHOP
BOILER BUILDING MACHINE SHOP
STORES
SHOP
ENTRANCE
OLD WORKS